A JEWISH APPRAISAL
OF DIALOGUE

Between Talk and Theology

G. David Schwartz

UNIVERSITY
PRESS OF
AMERICA

Lanham • New York • London

Copyright © 1994 by
University Press of America,® Inc.
4720 Boston Way
Lanham, Maryland 20706

3 Henrietta Street
London WC2E 8LU England

Library of Congress Cataloging-in-Publication Data

Schwartz, G. David.
A Jewish appraisal of dialogue : between talk and theology / by
G. David Schwartz.
p.   cm.
Includes bibliographical references and index.
1. Judaism—Relations—Christianity.   2. Christianity and other
religions—Judaism.   3. Dialogue—Religious aspects—Judaism.
4. Dialogue—Religious aspects—Christianity.   5. Jesus Christ—
Jewish interpretations.   I. Title.
BM535.S318   1994   296.3'872—dc20   93–40734 CIP

ISBN 0–8191–9413–1 (cloth : alk. paper)
ISBN 0–8191–9414–X (pbk. : alk. paper)

 The paper used in this publication meets the minimum requirements of
American National Standard for Information Sciences—Permanence
of Paper for Printed Library Materials, ANSI Z39.48–1984.

FOR GILDA

Contents

Preface

Depending on who you talk with, the relationship between Jews and Christians is declared to be an important concern, negligible, a fundamental aspect of daily existence, a necessary evil, at a critical juncture, or passe. And these are people who have, or had, some interest in dialogue. By far the majority of Jews and Christians have little or no interest in learning about an alien other. Life is difficult enough earning a living, instilling the proper values in our children, doing what has to be done, and hoping we are sufficiently alert to enjoy any leisure time we may be able to rescue from the realm of necessity.

The essays which follow assume, and were written from the advantage of, finding an escape from that which immediately has to be done. Understanding another takes time and, I will claim, is worth the effort. Our daily drudgery is made all the more treacherous because what we do with our free time too often resembles what we do as work. Frequently the same clock which guides our working hours determines our leisure activities -- we have to be at the stadium at a specific time, therefore dishes have to be done before we leave; the movie begins promptly at seven, therefore dinner has to be ready, served, finished, cleaned up, and the baby sitter in the house by 6:30, and so on.

Further, we design ruts for ourselves. The television is more attractive than going out for an evening. Going out is too expensive. Our friends have similar problems and worries which prevent our schedules from matching their own. When we do go out with them, because they are our friends, and because we do have similar worries and concerns, we spend time discussing our problems. We love them dearly. But they use the same language we do, focus on the same issues as we do, frequently draw the same conclusions we do. We eat at an elegant restaurant and discuss how expensive the evening is turning out to be, think about what we are missing on television, worry if any of our children have locked the baby sitter in the basement, feel nervous because we have to be up at a certain hour tomorrow morning to be at work, or at the stadium, a rehearsal, a recital.

If we want a pleasant row of azaleas up front, we must work at it. If we want a nice vegetable garden in back, we must work at it. A clean environment, both from room to room and in the living room of earth, takes work. Leisure requires work. The good life we envision privately and share with friends takes work.

We love our friends, love them dearly. But we know them too well. We know their concerns. They are the same as our own. Our friends are the same as we are. Our friends are us.

We are comfortable in our lives, too comfortable. Yet our leisure hours are at one and the same time tense and boring. Tense, because we are too hurried. Boring, because we do the same thing repeatedly, behave routinely, find our excitements too far between one another, too meager. There is so little surprise, so little to celebrate.

Each of us seek surprise and excitement in otherness. We crave that which is different and, because different, interesting and delightful. If a thing is too different, of course, we ignore it or fear it. But each life has some element of otherness which we celebrate. We have our individual tendencies which lead us to admire or even charm an entirely different world into existence. There may be many different worlds to celebrate: the paradoxical world of Franz Kafka, or Jorge Luis Borges, and comedic world of the Marx Brothers, or Jay Leno, the surrealistic world of Thomaso Landolfi or Salvador Dali, the world of Chagall, James Joyce, Mozart, the Beatles, Michelangelo, Frank Lloyd Wright, Batman, Stephen King, Martin Luther King, King Kong, and so on.

Participation in dialogue as an intellectual endeavor or a social adventure, an emotional event or a spiritual encounter is a way of creating a world. The conversations between Jews and Christians, whether it occurs in casual conversation at the work place, in a formalized study group, or in a little known journal, is as exciting as the participants' willingness to learn. The willingness to learn begins, perhaps, with the participants desire to state his or her convictions. Typically, response elicits response. This is not the case in our daily drudgery, where the code is to do a chore and get it over with, keep our mouths shut, our opinions to ourselves, our nose to the grindstone.

Dialogue thrives on what I think, depends on my opinion. This is unique! How can my opinion ever be boring?

The world which we create in dialogue is as tenuous or effective as we wish it to be. The world which we immediately compose can be as exciting and creative as we are willing to make it. The world can be a quarterly meeting or a daily challenge. When giving my conviction I elicit and learn from the statement of conviction of the other. Either of our thoughts may run the gamut from intuitive insight to studied scholarship. Neither of us need be conclusive. Tentative conversations are merely a promise to further discussions at a later date. The world, each of them, continues and grow with our participation.

The initial inspiration for the papers which follow are fairly apparent. Seven papers were the result of dialogue with authors. Three were the result of situations. Two were attempts to summarize and expand areas of concern. Yet the papers which follow are not occasional pieces. A particular occasion prompted each writing, but the occasion for effective relationship continues.

"On the Reluctance of Jews to Discuss Religious Truths" indicates that we Jews have no inherent reason to avoid dialogue. "Why Jews Ought to Engage in Dialogue" argues that we ought not avoid dialogue. "Expositions From the Lord's Table" discusses a text which, **while** written by a Christian for a Christian audience, is an example of the internal theological prospectus which is fairly common in the Western part of the world. Christians speaking to fellow Christians engage in a debate which we Jews ought not to disinterestedly watch. We ought to become involved. "Jewish-Christian Relations and the Thought of Samuel Sandmel" is an attempt to justify Jewish involvement in theological discussions.

"Confrontation or Conversation: Models for a Jewish-Christian Dialogue" suggests an attitude, we may even call it a methodological attitude, for approaching the other. While the term 'methodological attitude' sounds too disinterested, I suggest an agreeable approach to the insights of Judaism and Christianity proceed through narratives to which Jews and Christians are intellectually and emotionally committed. "Jews and Catholics Discussing Bible and Jesus" reports on the practice of dialogue by example of a particular evening which did not eschew the most "intense" issues. "Two Popular Jewish Interpretations of Jesus" purports to be a study of how *not* to engage in dialogue. "Is

There a Jewish Reclamation of Jesus?" is a different approach to the question of how we ought to integrate honesty and integrity while taking the ultimate concerns of the other seriously. Chapter Eight shows how we can learn even from those with whom we have the most fundamental disagreements.

A different track is taken from Chapter Nine on. "Rosenzweigian Meditations," as the title may suggest, is an effort to deal with several themes in a casual manner. The informal tone of the paper seemed more conducive to a candid discussion which would otherwise have required several papers cast in a more scholarly framework. "Rosenzweigian Meditations" is a practice of what I identify as Franz Rosenzweig's "literal dialectic." The paper seems to be argued from a Jewish perspective. Obviously it is, but the genesis of the paper derives from a remark one Christian friend made to another at a discussion group. He said, "Why do they call it re-judaization? Why don't they just call it what it is? Authentic Christianity!" "Noahide Laws, Christian Covenants, and Jewish Expectations" argues that Christianity stands in an authentic covenant with God and spells out what I take to be the consequences of that fact. "A Note on the Friends of Israel and the Jews" argues that we ought to pay attention to our public attitude and modify our short-term criticism with an eye toward the long-term advantages we expect. "Scratch a Goy" is a harsh paper on which to end. In this chapter, I argue that the Jewish attitude toward Christian peoples is deplorable. In doing so, however, I follow the examples which extend from Abraham arguing with God, through the contentions of our sages, our rabbis, our scholars, our neighbors, our friends, and our families. A friend once joked: We Jews do not have guardian angels; we have *nebbishes* ["busy-bodies"]. Without a doubt, those I deal with most critically, including Rabbi Novak, Father Pawlikowski, Reverend Van Buren, are the very same people from whom I have learned the most.

If we Jews are loath to speak about Christianity (Chapter One) and obnoxious when we speak about abstract Christians (Chapter Twelve) -- "abstract" because some of our best friends are Christian, and our friends are certainly not like the others -- we require another attitude entirely. *A Jewish Appraisal of Dialogue* is a first practice of the attitude which is recommended. The attitude includes self-interest and self-preservation. I argue in the following that Jewish self-preservation is most coherently founded in relationship with others. To relate in a coherent manner requires sensitivity and honesty, recognition of distinctions and similarities, speaking of our concerns and recognizing the concerns of the other as well. I would also claim that responding to the call to tell about ourselves, which is an agency for learning about ourselves and others, is a significant break in routine. Growth is exciting and important. To engage in dialogue with a significant other is to treat the other as a friend along the road we travel and to help create a world most conducive to the good life we seek.

Acknowledgements

A number of years ago, conversations with Mark Cullinan and Lori Stanton raised issues and concerns which the enclosed papers only partially address. I do not know if my responses to their conversations had any effect on them, but consideration of the questions and problems they raised gave directly to my intellectual interests and focus to my social concerns.

I have benefitted from frequent conversations with Rabbi Gershom Barnard of Northern Hills Synagogue-Congregation B'nai Avraham. Often without knowing the extent of his influence, Rabbi Barnard probed issues, challenged my thinking and offered suggestions and alternatives which will not necessarily find him in agreement with the enclosed, but upon which he certainly had a positive effect.

Several conversations with Mary Lou Vera, Ecumenical Officer of the Cincinnati Archdiocese, were equally challenging and probing. Ms. Vera, like all the participants in the Catholic-Jewish Dialogue group, asked questions and made statements which required that I think beyond the hitherto acceptable. Ms. Vera has always been most helpful and forthcoming with insights, information and suggestions.

I am in debt to Sister Ruth Graf, R.S.M. and Dr. Arthur Dewey, Th.D., creators of the "Deadly Memories" seminar at Xavier University. Participation in the seminar brought me into contact with a number of intelligent and thoughtful people who, again, have influenced the pages which follow.

Dr. Michael Cook from Hebrew Union College has been most helpful in giving freely of his time and good advice.

Also, I thank the participants of Northern Hills Synagogue, St. Bartholomew Church, and St. John-St. Matthew United Church of Christ tri-alogue between Jews, Catholics and Protestants. In comfortable settings, guided by the extraordinary scholarship and sensitivity of Rabbi Barnard, Father Tom DiFolco and Rev. Craig McClellan, the most intense and potentially explosive issues were faced with humor, understanding, and loving-kindness.

Technical assistance and location of otherwise inaccessible information and sources has graciously been supplied on a number of occasions by Hebrew Union College staff member, and excellent friend of the family, Laurel S. Wolfson. Laurel also stepped in to type the final version of this text when technology proved not to be as advanced as we would like it to be.

Finally, and always, I thank my wife Gilda for her patience and understanding with regard to my studies and ideas. We do not always agree, and thus are an excellent example of the relationship espoused in these pages. This book is dedicated to Gilda.

In spite of all the good advice and assistance which has been my good fortune to receive, all remaining mistakes and errors are my corresponding misfortune.

"Is There a Jewish Reclamation of Jesus?" was previously published in the Journal of Ecumenical Studies (Vol. 24, No. 1, Winter 1987), copyright 1987. Used by permission.

"Confrontation or Conversation: Models for a Jewish-Christian Dialogue" was previously published in Encounter (Vol. 50, No. 2, Spring 1989).

"Jews and Catholics Discussing Bible and Jesus" was previously published in The University of Dayton Review (Vol. 20, No. 1, Summer 1989).

"Jewish-Christian Relations and the Thought of Samuel Sandmel" was previously published in Ecumenical Trends (Vol. 18, No. 11, December 1989).

"Noahide Laws, Christian Covenants, and Jewish Expectations" appeared in a slightly different version in the Journal of Ecumenical Studies (Vol. 27, No. 4, Fall 1990), copyright 1991. Used by permission.

Portions of Chapter Ten originally appeared as a review in Jewish Spectator (Vol. 56, No. 4, Spring 1992).

All biblical citations, unless otherwise indicated, are from The New English Bible. The Delegates of the Oxford University and the Syndics of the Cambridge University Press, 1961, 1970, 1989. Reprinted by permission.

Chapter 1

On the Reluctance of Jews to Discuss Religious Truths

Father Richard W. Rousseau, in his introduction to the collection of essays entitled *Christianity and Judaism: The Deepening Dialogue*, refers to the Jewish reluctance to discuss "questions of religious truth" (Rousseau, 25). Father Rousseau is correct to refer to this reluctance as an historical characteristic of the Jewish people. The rabbinic traditions as recorded in the Talmud and Midrashim, of course, do present polemical points which respond to the issues raised by sectarian or non-Jewish views. However, it is reasonable to say that these remarks were intended for internal consumption and study. They were not primarily asserted as remarks which were to be overheard by any people other than the rabbis or their disciples.

What one says at home may not be the same as what one is willing to say in the public domain. This fact, however, ought to be regarded as tact and sensitivity rather than hypocrisy. As an alternative, the reluctance of Jews to speak of religious truth in the Middle Ages may be attributed to fear of persecution. This was the case in spite of the exceptions which occurred at the public disputes commanded to take place in Barcelona, Tortosa, and elsewhere. If the reluctance of the Jews to speak on topics of religious truth is not quite true, yet not false, in the cases of the rabbinic Jew and the medieval Jew, we are confronted with the testimony of the contemporary Jew.

There are many Synagogue-Church groups which meet in order to exchange polite information about the traditions, practices and perceptions of the respective groups involved. In these discussions,

1

however, there is a natural conditioning which prevents, as it should, violent or heated exchange. Anger is left for the theologians. Among the lay people, especially those not familiar with their synagogue or church participation at these neighborhood discussion groups, ignorance or indifference keeps them from discussing religious truths. The more scholarly, if you will, among Jews do not seek confrontation for two, contradictory, reasons.

First, and I assume the same may be said about the intelligent Christian, there does not seem to be much reason to debate the truth inasmuch as the religious person supposes he or she possesses sufficient truth. Second, as Father Rousseau says, why stir up a hornets' nest? In other words, why fight about that which is either unimportant or beyond debate. The purpose of this paper is both to show why I consider these two points to be contradictory, and to thrash my way through the thicket which surrounds the issues of religious dialogue and emotional need.

As to the first point, there seems to be a fundamental conflict between the "necessary" espousal of the fact that I possess the truth and the alternative. The option is simply that I do not possess the truth, and this would be too much for any person to live with. A way around this choice may be sought in an analysis of religion as something other than a concern with truth content. But if religion is not concerned with truth values, then religion becomes a question of psychology, or cultural relativism, or some other subjective, and therefore changeable (and therefore inconsequential) ideology or behavior. If we grant on the one hand that there are subtle yet distinct differences between Judaism and Christianity which makes the claim of "whole truth" for the one an implicit disclaimer of the truth of the other, we must grant on the other hand that the God who is the focus of each religion is identical. God is neither mutable nor inconsequential. God is, in the Western tradition a Being greater than which none can be conceived. God is eternal, Omnipotent, Omniscient, and so on.

Yet the Western idea of God also holds that God is personally concerned with both humanity and myself, the universal and the particular. Perhaps it is only the case that when God is inferred to be concerned with my holding the truth that my need to espouse the truth is important. Luckily, the Judeo-Christian tradition is committed to the idea that God is involved with much more than my simply believing the pure facts (as if we could know these). God is also concerned with my livelihood, my soul, and my being true to both my fellow human beings and my feelings towards being itself.

Were God not concerned for my current condition and my future existence, it would not only be the case that my suggestion that you are in possession of truth implies that I am not, but it would follow that I alienate myself from the eternal truth which is God, or in God's providence. When we consider the birds in the sky, they have neither thoughts or beliefs, yet God feeds and protects them. Still, unless and until the human condition changes drastically, men and women will continue to espouse the idea that they possess the truth if that which they assert is different from what any other person assumes. The other person, however honorable, must be thought to be misguided. We would all agree that genuine dialogue cannot be based on conflict, but it is precisely our commonly held beliefs which prevent religion from being a form of psychology or, from that common perspective, a relative issue.

Let us consider the personal God of our common tradition. If the question I am about to ask sounds blasphemous, it may only be because we do not take God's personal involvement sufficiently serious. My question stems from the thought that any conflict between groups of people sets a precedent which may be used to heighten the conflict, and thereby make our discussion, our search for truth, more difficult. The insinuation that I am right, or that you are wrong, or vice versa, in religious tradition -- as long as we are faithful to ourselves, our people, and our God -- is misguided. Moreover, such conviction is destructive. Here is the question: God may be eternal, but need God be boring? Can we really conceive of a superior being who desires that everyone either believe or, within a broad scope, perform in an identical manner? If this were how God intended the human world, we would expect to have been created to act, and perhaps look, the same. We would all, because we would be true children of God, espouse the eternal truth, have perfectly shaped chins, and act like versions of robots with a peculiar free will which functions in perfect harmony with the divine plan. If God were boring, nature and nurture would have been without variance, and conflicts would never arise. If God expected crushing obedience, as opposed to moral obedience, God would be boring in the sense indicated above. God would not, in other words, be the supreme being.

The fact that sameness is not the way of the world, and is not the way of nature, suggests that it is not the way of God. Indeed, there are suggestions in the Bible that God does not expect anything like a totalitarian regime to unify people as subjects and children. Isaiah speaks about traditional enemies becoming reconciled:: "In that day, Israel shall rank with Egypt and Assyria, those three, and shall be a blessing in the center of the world" (Isa. 19:24). Equal ranking clearly denies submergence into a single entity. The so-called Hebrew God is concerned for all nations, as is evident by the prophetic concern with the behaviors of those nations (see Amos 1:3-2:3). Jonah, for example, is sent to a Gentile nation in order to preach repentance, not conversion to Judaism. Again, Cyrus, King of Persia, is hailed as God's very own "messiah" (Isa. 45:1), for he performed the work of the Lord.

The prophet Joel speaks an interesting and relevant prophecy concerning the End of Days. Joel says in God's name: "I will pour out my spirit upon all flesh, and your sons and your daughters will prophesize" (Joel 3:1). The question arises, if God's spirit is poured out on all people, what need is there of prophecy? I suggest the meaning of this verse is that even during the time when God is both universally recognized and ubiquitously regarded as the Father/Mother, the many people who have cognizance of God will find the diverse interpretations of other people of interest, and request to hear their insights and perspectives. The End of Days, in this view, begins to take on the tones and hues of an end to jealousy and spiritual competition. And if this is not the precise purpose of engagement in dialogue, I cannot imagine what is.

I suggest an alternative understanding than that which may compel one to question why Jews do not engage in discussion of religious truth. I do not pretend to speak for all Jews, nor any Jew aside from myself. We do not possess the truth. Life is, in an abrupt, ambiguous phrase, a dialectic. Knowledge and behavior are ever closer approximations of the eternal, immutable truth. Knowledge and action create us anew through diversity and change. Our non-possession of truth, which must cause both humility and curiosity, constitutes the highest reason for reluctance to discuss questions of religious truth. To assume that we possess the truth in toto would be equivalent to the assertion that we possessed God's spirit fully. Yet, as Joel indicates, even at the End of Days we will be in need of more than ourselves and our own visions.

In spite of this dialectical distance from ultimate truth, or perhaps because of it, dialogue between disagreeing partners is evermore necessary. I assume that all who at least participate in dialogue on some level will agree that benefit is derived from our discussions. I offer a personal, if long-term and idealistic, opinion of the benefit which may be expected from genuine conversation. To paraphrase a rabbinic teaching: discussion leads to understanding, understanding leads to cooperation, which leads to resolution of problems, which then leads to harmony and peace, which directs us towards time for higher pursuits which, one trusts, leads to saintliness.

It is an error, perhaps even blasphemy, to say there is no truth. It is, however, both fair and reasonable to says there is no agreement today about the fundamental truth which unifies and makes cogent all of the human paths stretching towards piety. Discussion of issues in terms of truth, then, are at best always penultimate. These issues may not be solved, and if dialogue is based on truth-content, dialogue will always be tentative. Hence, discussion on all levels, from the conversation between acquaintances meeting on the street, to writings in scholarly journals, ought to proceed not on the basis of what we do or do not possess, do or do not feel to be true. Dialogue, speech and discussion, ought to proceed on the paradoxical basis of what ought to be done, beginning, perhaps, with what ought to be done to resolve ignorance and ill-will among non-participants. The issues of Jewish-Christian relations, as I understand the problem, is how we can aid each other into saintliness.

We cannot speak in absolutes. Yet if we proceed as if we are unable to discuss our perceptions of truth, we run the risk of either ignoring these larger issues or, more subtly and more perversely, permit erosion of strongly held beliefs. In any event, we set a bad precedent. On the other hand, assertion of religious truths, of highly held values, is precisely to act somewhat in the manner of prophets and to stir up a hornets' nest. Minimally, the prophetic mission was to challenge complacency. We remember that Satan, the adversary, is in the Book of Job (and other, less well known parts of Hebraic literature) as a trusted agent of God. If God is indeed not boring, and even takes delight in viewing the dialectic of life as we live it, then it seems to be the case that God enjoys both conflict and resolution. Several tales in the Talmud speak about God's satisfaction that sagacious children had "defeated" divinity in the area of intellectual dialectics. It seems to be our task, then, to keep God interested in us. We can do this through our mutual search for contemporary righteousness.

In terms of the Christian query for Jewish discussion of religious truth, the Christian ought to understand that there is a peculiar problem with regard to the Jewish participant's part of the conversation which the Christian does not face. Needless to say, the Jew does not regard this peculiarity as a problem. The issue may be presented in any of several ways, but the following examples partake of the particular understanding which resides with every Jew who discusses "religion." Jews have been taught by the earliest sages that all expression which is for the sake of heaven is legitimate. Even when the sages disagreed with their opponents, they recognized their words too were the words of the living God. The Talmud is replete with contradictory ideas and opinions, but this was not viewed as debilitating. Indeed, contradictions were retained to inspire the search for deeper, reconciling expressions. Here, as elsewhere, conflict leads to resolution. Jews also believe that what is essential is not talk, but action. It is not our ideas which will benefit the world, but our performing towards righteousness. In the volume which Father Rousseau edited, Clark M. Williamson stated, following R. Travers Herford, that "Judaism was and is a behavioral system, having no creed. It was an orthopraxy - the very thing Jesus is said to have demanded" (Rousseau, 150).

The emphasis on doing as opposed to "speculating" helps explain the annoying habit of the Jew to rely on historical records in ecumenical discussion. To be sure, there is quite a bit of speculation in historical research. But for the most part, history is the document of what has been accomplished. History is, by and large, a record of facts. Jews do no profess to know what the God of surprise will do next.

I have referred to God as not boring, as the God of surprise. The Jewish idea of God is promulgated to closely align divine being with the human condition. God is not only ultimately responsible for the conditions of human life, but a participant. God, then, while an eternal entity, is at the same time operating in history in an intimate manner. There is no third point which synthesizes or concludes this paradox. God, as conceived by the Jews, understands that human beings cannot function with perceptions which are, so to speak, beyond the human level. Nor does God (being just and merciful) require human beings to behave awkwardly. There is, on the other hand, am implicit demand in life to continually develop and advance beyond our current human powers of insight and appreciation. This is, however, a separate paradox. I mention God's participation in history as further evidence of the Jewish proclivity to expound historical issues. Insofar as the Christian has an interest to discuss that which transcends history, the

Jew perceives the Christian request as contradictory (but not debilitating). The discussion of religious truths, the Jew holds, begins with, and stays close to, discussion of historical issues and temporary cognitive truths as applied to daily routine.

I do not argue, as suggested by Maimonides, HaLevi and other Jewish sages, that Christianity is slightly inferior to Judaism but exists as an entity in its own right. Nor do I argue, as suggested by Buber, Rosenzweig and more contemporary Jewish philosophers, that Judaism and Christianity stand equally justified before God in a manner that is both astounding and paradoxical. Both Judaism and Christianity, I claim, are modes of life in the contemporary search for God through the approximation of truth. Both Judaism and Christianity have developed broad categories of revelation (whether they are called halacha or dogmatics), yet each demand we listen for God's voice in our daily life. Is Judaism chosen religion? Yes. Is Christianity? Yes. For what have they been chosen? To seek God and witness the findings of their independent searches. To seek God and live.

Henry Seigman, expresses what plausibly seems like the contrary to our topic of reluctance to speak religious truth. Seigman expresses the telling self-criticism of Jews that we have been "somewhat less than daring in initiating a process of self-examination" (Rousseau, 165). The suggestion implies that Jews have indeed been speaking about ultimate issues, but have been talking strictly as if they possessed the exclusive truth.

Although two specimens do not a species make, a book written by a contemporary Rabbi carries a similar determination about Jewish reluctance to discuss religious ideas. Harvey Falk says that, "Jews are traditionally reticent to discuss other religions, and especially Christianity" (Falk, 12). This seems a curious statement in a text which is fundamentally an analysis of Rabbi Eliezer's relation with Jewish-Christians (ca. 80 C.E.), Rabbi Jacob Emden's views on the founders of Christianity (ca. 1750), and the historical understandings of the Talmudic statements concerning other religions. Indeed, although phrased in hyperbolic, perhaps even sarcastic language, we would have an interesting monograph if we analyzed the plethora of comments the rabbis made not only about the Jewish-Christians, but about the heathen peoples who surrounded them. It will at last be seen that the rabbis did not refrain from speaking their mind. And whether with good or ill acceptance, this freedom to assert is essential to dialogue, and a prerequisite to gaining knowledge.

The sense of "frustrated dialogue" shared by both Rabbi Falk and Father Rousseau certainly needs to be qualified. Jews are, to be sure, unwilling to debate Christians; but at the same time they seem to relish the process of getting to know the view of the other, or the terms of comparison. Jews are glad to share subjective perspectives and compare or contrast creedal or ideological statements. During inter-faith meetings, in other words, Jews are happy to bolster popular conceptions of their belief with exemplic stories of friends and incidents of which they have heard. It may be the case that the majority of Jews, and I assume a majority of Christians, do not find access to scholarly journals. If this is the problem, rather than the popular discussions which do occur both at the work-place and between synagogues and churches, then it seems we are not dealing with the problem of inter-faith interest, but the different issue of generating a larger commitment to scholarly research.

Scholars, to be sure, search for truth and understanding. Insofar as my contention that each religion approximates truth, but does not possess truth, would appear to assert a form of eclecticism, I no doubt offend the integrity felt by each religious participant. Perhaps the erroneous impression of relativism cannot be overcome until we learn, in the words of Frederick Franck, that there "is no Christian, Buddhist, Hindu, or Judaic truth. There is Truth/Reality - and there is delusion" (Franck, 286). It should be obvious that such an all-encompassing, ubiquitous truth can only be expressed in particular movements if it is to make sense to us. Insofar as these diverse assertions conflict, we need reasoned discussions and commitments to the process of understanding in order to insure that our controversies are "for the sake of heaven."

I have dealt with paradoxes throughout this paper, and wish to conclude with this final one. The situation is like the one in the old Jewish joke where the jurist determines that the prosecution is right, and also determines that the defense is right, and the bystander who objects to this strange decision is also right. We ought not speak about "truth" as if we possessed it, yet we do and cannot help but do so. Again, we cannot have genuine discussions until we are able to express our innermost doubts, when, that is, we are far from debating religious truths and are greatly involved with seeking more penetrating approximations towards resolving doubts. This state of affairs would seem to a few to be possible only when Jews and Christians, and all other peoples, belong to a single religious entity. But we know this is neither possible nor desirable. Further, as I trust the prophets teach us, it is not necessary.

What is necessary, it seems, is honest disagreement, and the understanding that beyond any disagreement is our similar quest for quality life under the auspices of living traditions and diverse cultures. Wrapped around all this like a bow, as it were, is the living God who refuses to be boring.

Chapter 2

Why Jews Ought to Engage In Dialogue

From a Jewish perspective, there are two reasons Jews ought to engage in dialogue with non-Jews. The first reason is to explain to non-Jews, in words and deed, how we are like them. The second reason is to explain to them, in words and deed, how we differ. In each case I assume that a Jew in word and deed is behaving as a self-respecting Jew.

It is necessary, perhaps, in a world which values similarity, to show we are comparable or related. Again, it is necessary, in a world which values individuality and distinctiveness, to show we are unique. This is not an argument that the world as we know it is composed of diverse expectations and behaviors. That much is obvious. Our prophets, however, envisioned a world where we Jews would show our uniqueness precisely in a world where the peoples of the nations value conformity, and we would show our likeness where the peoples value drastic individualism. The prophets envisioned the world as the one in which they lived. Thus, the Hebrew, Israelite, Jewish people were required to be beacons of contention or, better, controversy. Perhaps this "prophetic recognition" contributed to our very own literature's reference to us as "stiff-necked." We Jews were almost *designed* to be burdens or, better, disturbing.

Nevertheless, we Jews were told we were to be a "holy people," "a nation of priests" to the Master of the Universe. We seem to have been chosen to walk the ways of strife while supporting, and being supported by, a code which professed to tell us the ways of right action and right thought. We were, through our own internal consistency, to

11

influence the people of the world. We were not, it should be noted, to convert the world to Judaism. Our influence was to extend to recognition of the one God and efficacious behavior towards our fellow human beings.

If so, the prophetic vision of our quarrelsomeness was, is, and will be destined to become something entirely different than that which may have been used as an excuse for our victimization. In the world to come, the world we will make out of our world, we Jews -- and others with us -- will be free to show uniqueness because diversity will be recognized to be of value. In such a world, people ought also be free to show their similarity. We are speaking about a changed world wherein we should fear neither our contrariness, nor the variance of being another, nor fear agreements that are compromises. We Jews were commissioned in part, it seems, to live the abolition of both radical, unhealthy individualism as well as untrue and dysfunctional totalisms. I can think of no place where the vision of this "future world" occurs with more success than in dialogues with those who are "like us in being not like us."

Jews ought to engage in dialogue with non-Jews, especially Christian people (although the differences between various sects and faith communities are great) because the abstract entity which goes under that name is the dominant presence in the Western world in which we live. There are Jews who live in parts of the world where dialogue might be undertaken with a majority population which is Muslim, Hindu, Buddhist, or another. In that precious state where we Jews are the majority, it is necessary for Jews to engage in dialogue with Jews.

To put it bluntly, without any dialectical subtlety, we ought to show the dominant majority we are like them so as to insure they befriend, defend, and protect us from *themselves*! Compared with the apocalyptic vision just enunciated, however, this eliciting of support and defence seems an inferior reason for dialogue. Nevertheless, it is adequate, if only barely, for initiating and maintaining dialogic friendship (that is, friendships which begin on the premise of the need for all participants to learn and be taught by others; where adult education is, if you will, the primary motivation for the occurrence of weekly, monthly, or at least regularly scheduled inter-faith dialogues). The question of social friendships is not presently addressed. For some Jews, social friendships with Christians are a moot point, for others a horror.

The idea that we Jews ought to maintain dialogue with another, or they with us, is too facile if reasoned as we Jews being their root. Neither contemporary Jews nor modern Christians are so thoroughly rooted in Torah, Talmud or New Testament. The bottom line is that we Jews need dialogue because we need protection. We need to show, as perhaps our grandparents may have stated it, the "potential murderer" that we are like them. If we were not here to be despised perhaps they would be next; if we were respected, perhaps they would be more respected among their kind. It is a conceit to add that righteous gentiles need our support and protection as well.

Our responsibility, in inter-religious dialogue no less than in daily life among fellow synagogue members, is to finesse the other to respect and, perhaps, admire us. I grant you that it is rarely stated so curtly. Nevertheless, our mothers and fathers have made many statements which when boiled down come to this statement: affirm yourself in a pleasant manner so that you will be affirmed by the others. Our task in inter-faith conversation seems to be to teach, to learn, and to show that while our "ideologies" (beliefs, principles of discourse and action, philosophies, culture, theologies) are difference, our social ethics are more similar than not.

Our social goals, which may justly be called "prophetic social ethics," will suggest that Judaism is not a stagnant entity, and perhaps that Christianity is not as complete as some would like to believe. Both Jews and Christians are commissioned -- covenanted, they used to say -- to alleviate the misery of the poor, protect the widow and orphan, to comfort the sick and contribute to our advance toward the good life. Who knows? If Isaiah were writing in our contemporary world of technology, world-wide communications and rapid transport, perhaps he would add that the sons *and daughters* of God are supposed to *end* poverty, cause suffering to *cease*, to *house* the homeless, *expel* the perceived need for recreational drugs, and *enhance* the development of leisure time and allow for an increase in personal creativity. The prophet may caution the contemporary person of Jewish, Christian or other background to end the miserable cycle of insensitivity and contribute to a new cycle of emotional, psychological, and physical improvement through better nutrition, more access to/interest in educational material, and a healthy respect for that which is essential for the advancement of all beings.

This over-brief, too speculative, announcement of "prophetic social ethics" as *our* ethics, not those of the prophets alone, suggests that our ideological difference are (a) not socially constricting, (b) not as essential as we may think (our parents said that actions speak louder than words); and (c) not the primary concern which makes our community worth engaging in battle. Our mutual social ethics -- perhaps summarily called the pursuit and attainment of justice in all her guises -- should keep us too busy to do battle.

It may be obvious that such identity does not lend itself to compromise. Jews should never compromise their faith, nor should Christians. Nor does striving toward justice -- the giving of money, the giving of time, acts of friendship, the kindness shown another, the protest for fair legal codes and practices, the standing up for what is right because it is correct, no matter who is to benefit -- admit of compromise. To strive for justice is essential. To change one's ideology, or deeply held belief, is but a personal use of time.

Far too many opportunities in life are missed because we become fascinated with viewing differences as a negative endowment. Too much is considered to be black or white, gender specific, or ethnically confirmed. This fascination, especially when it occurs without even the pretense of self-understanding, is dangerous. It has generally been the case that one set of differences -- always the *other* -- needs to be cut down to size, imprisoned, rejected or eliminated. There does, however, seem to be a higher realism which is more properly concerned with our deepest convictions. This higher realism may be motivated by the ultimate difference -- the difference between God and the human -- or may be motivated by the simple perception of the plethora of manifold complexities in even the simplest species of animal, plant or mineral. The higher realism is attained with the realization that I personally, or myself in community, am one among the many. Harmony is obtained when we not only recognize differences but celebrate them. A celebration of differences which, as noted, recognizes our own difference as well, is not only not threatening, but is an act of ennoblement, is life enhancing, self-nurturing and offers potential for creative efforts. The higher realism draws us up!

We have already begun explicating the second reason Jews ought to engage in dialogue. Conversation with another precisely when the other is in the process of being *another* allows *me* to be his or her other. Hearing a Christian explain that they believe X because of reasons a, b, and c allows Jews to affirm that they do not believe X, or that they believe Y (or that they too believe X, but for reasons d, e, and f). The primacy of similar social ethics should not allow hostility or bitterness to ascend. The explanations concerning why Jews or Christians believe X or Y or Z is an advancement over the historic instances where the Jew or Christian supposed the other believed something or other, hazily expressed and surely obnoxious, for reasons which were thought not only invalid, but evil.

Hearing a Christian talk about his or her belief in Jesus allows us Jews to better appreciate our non-acceptance of Jesus. Dialogue affords the opportunity for us to get clear about ourselves as we get clear about the other. The Christian believer telling us what a Christian believes is certainly more advantageous than hearing from one of our own what we merely suppose Christians believe. The possibility of distortion, misrepresentation, and trivialization is minimized. In dialogue, it is interesting to hear Christians putting their best foot forward, so to speak, and Jews putting their best foot forward as well. (There are, it turns out -- although Christianity is more successful than we Jews at keeping such knowledge "out of press" -- non-believing Christians. Perhaps this is indicative that community, the doings of society, are more important than belief-systems.)

The advantage of hearing the truths of another expressed and commented upon is doubled by our ability to find more creative ways of announcing our beliefs and their reasons. Dialogue with the significant other allows us one more opportunity to become *better Jews*! Hearing about and celebrating the heritage of another allows us to recognize our own different heritage and appreciate it more than perhaps we did going into dialogue. Dialogue offers us a nuance of understanding our own tradition which is certainly not afforded in the bleak classroom after "regular" school, or from adult professionals with a thesis to defend. Hearing one's wife, one's husband, one's neighbor, one's children explicate the legacy of Judaism is often surprising and frequently enlightening.

We may be instructed, but are rarely educated when we are told only about ourselves. Was your Hebrew school instruction as boring as mine? Learning may advance best by comparisons, yet it is true that we were rarely, if ever, instructed in any aspect of Christianity. When we are told about Christianity as children, we learned nothing of the

Christian heritage and traditions. We learn only about their involvement -- frequently negative, rarely positive -- in the history of the Jewish people.

I have argued that the social ethics of Jews and Christians are similar, and take priority over our diverse beliefs. Nevertheless, I have indicated that there is an essential need for inter-faith conversations, and that such discussions are primarily concerned with statements of belief. I do not think my position is paradoxical if dialogue, while concentrating on beliefs and inevitably showing the historical and psychological reasons behind beliefs, either shows beliefs as secondary values or shows, on the other hand, how they motivate both Jews and Christians to efficacious social behavior. Further, my position would be contradictory if I were making the epistemological point that differences are essential to recognizing truth (a popular philosophical position which, luckily, I need not address). I would ultimately be subject to the criticism that my distinction between social practice and inter-faith discussion was not epistemically sound. But I do not make an epistemological point. I make an *attitudinal* point. We shall always have differences between us (that is something to be celebrated)! Nevertheless, the *attitude* with which we approach those differences is definitive.

We may look upon the difference between Christians and Jews (or between Jews and Jews) as a fact to bemoan. The mournful attitude affects our behavior negatively. We note difference and begin looking for causes and solutions. If, as I argue, differences are by and large not a problem (unless, of course, they are debilitating or dangerous because they detract from progress toward the good life), there is no need for solutions. If diversity will always be with us, there need be no solutions because there is no problem. Further, the issue of identifying differences as a negative encumberment, if there is a "problem" of differences in other words, ultimately leads to the question of who is right, who is superior, who should dominate, who should assert their presumed licit rights to mastery. In a world where human beings have nuclear capabilities -- the same human beings who are in charge of, or should be in charge of, the environment -- we must search for a perspective, an attitude, beyond epistemological blindness or differential mastery.

As an alternative to the attempt at obliterating the difference, our attitude may be one of ignoring the diversity, or "tolerating" the deviations. I claim, echoing Sartre, that refusal to make a decision with regard to variance -- by which I mean anything less than *celebrating* difference -- allows others to make the decision with regard to the variegated. The result is, *at best*, that things continue the way they have been which, we might agree if we look at the cycle of events which surround us, is not great.

The third option, the cogent practice of prophetic social ethics in word and deed, would seem to allow us the proper attitude to face the challenges of life and offer effective responses. We ought to undertake the celebration of difference *for our own sake*. I do not claim this is a "natural" attitude, nor is it easily obtained. The attitudinal point which is at issue requires fortitude and tenacity. We require an effort at personal courage and an educational commitment to extend our Jewish knowledge into communal comparisons and verbal modesty. The attitude requires we overcome the negative perception of differences and find dignity in diversity.

Of course, the excuses to refrain from the effort are numerous. Our own Jewish education is not what we wish it were. Time constraints are rampant. Energy is sapped. These are each great reasons to allow personal mental laziness, the continuation of inter-communal misunderstanding, and the limping on of the world as we know it.

It has not been my intention to slight personal belief. I know from my own experience that beliefs run the gamut from those intensely held to those of a fleeing, curious nature. I do assert that beliefs, while interesting in terms of discussion and clarification, are of a secondary nature. Life is primary, doing is essential, and -- as an extension beyond this merely existential and possibly trivial point -- seeking the good life is fundamental. Recognizing the secondary status of beliefs frees us to actively pursue the good life.

Concerning relations between Jews and Christians, perhaps even more so between Jews and Jews, placing belief in the paramount position leads to arguments and belligerence. I believe every Jew has the right and obligation to say, "My ideas and opinions are coherent and proper." I believe every Christian has an equal right and obligation. Stated without a context my assertion is either a paradox or relativistic, or both. In the context I have attempted to design, beliefs are motivational, which means they are in service to a higher goal, which is proper action. A belief which cannot stimulate the believer to proper action is a useless thought. A belief which does not submit to reasonable discussion and educational opportunities is like an unopened book.   Finally, a belief which does not allow dissimilar beliefs the identical status as motivational and prophetically oriented to social ethics is a failure.   For beliefs to succeed, they should be secondary.   Proper activities speak louder about my beliefs than mere words.

Jesus, in a sermon which includes the words "Be careful not to make a show of your religion" (Matthew 6:1), also states that his disciples will recognize the character of people by their fruits (7:15-20).   Likewise, a midrash in <u>Genesis Rabbah</u> says the fruit trees were asked why they made no noise.   The trees replied, "Our fruits are sufficient advertisement."   These assertions suggest the ultimate reason Jews ought to engage in dialogue: because on a non-verbal level we already do dialogue in some sense!   We ought to make our assertions, our character, conscious and creative.

Chapter Three

Expositions From The Lord's Table: Typology and Midrash

If it is the case, as Jean Paul Richter asserted, that a scholar knows no boredom, it is mostly because scholars have inquisitive minds which refuse to rest. This is a generous consideration. Others may say that scholars search until they find a viewpoint which bests their contemporaries, fans their egotism into the future, or they simply enjoy beating dead horses. Yet every field has favorite issues which can captivate active minds and refuse to deliver a definitive opinion.

In New Testament scholarship, one of the more tempting of questions is whether or not the Last Supper was a Passover Seder. Arguments have generally proceeded in terms of textual and/or chronological analyses between the Synoptic texts and the Book of John. Scholars given to quantitative analysis may itemize the ritual objects (bread rather than matzah, bitter herbs, four cups of wine, etc.) which either were or were not present at the meal Jesus shared with his disciples. Gillian Feeley-Harnik, in The Lord's Table (1981); has essayed a delicious text wherein she argues not only that the relics of the Seder were present (in transcendence, as it were) but that the procession of the meal (in an eschatological sense) adheres to the Jewish ceremony. Never mind the fact that the Seder is not a relic, and eschatological and transcendant only in a minor sense.

Our author's presentation of the anthropological case that Judaism increasingly identified God's word with food, so that dietary regulations disproportionately came to represent Torah, and violations of dietary requirements most exclusively equated apostasy, is excellently

19

presented, informative and interesting. The ecological and economic aspects of food were closely tied to the theology of Judaism. Indeed, Feeley-Harnik's point is that food is fundamentally theological. She says, each of the prophets, including Jesus, "pleaded for the rights of the literally as well as the spiritually hungry" (168). In prophetic thought, one's attitude toward the hungry, as well as the orphaned and poor, was indicative of one's attitude toward God. Hence, within limits, it is "spiritual" or "righteous" to give one's food away rather than ingest it. In the case of Jesus, however, the dialectic between theology and the hunger is given at least one eschatological transmutation ("The poor you will always have with you" -- Matt. 26:11). The prophets, who did not have the sociological End of the World confronting them, were more demanding that one can only be righteous if their actions included giving food to the poor (see Ezek. 18:5-9; Isa. 58:7). One was even commanded to give bread to a hungry enemy (Prov. 25:21). It is safe to say that, according to Judaism, hunger is a sin.

We may begin to investigate *The Lord's Table* as a form of typological exposition. If metaphor may loosely be described as likening an earlier phenomenon to a latter (creative; parabolic) phenomenon, then typology may be described as metaphor in reverse. The concrete item is not, in typology, the one which is made into a parable. Rather, the concrete is taken to be that which was announced by the prior parable. Ursula Bruman says the type is a special sort of symbol, a prophetic symbol, where the "image is historically given in the Old Testament and the meaning must be inferred as the 'fulfillment' of the image in a certain direction" (Bruman, 24). Long ago, Melito had said, "the model indeed existed, but then the reality appeared" (see Hall, 5). In sum, traditional Christian exegesis treats the "Old Testament" as a clue to the reality which was to manifest itself in the life of Jesus and the Church.

I have suggested above that Feeley-Harnik treats the Last Supper in an eschatological sense. More properly, the Last Supper is treated in a unique manner as a form of typological exegesis. The Last Supper is presented as a story wherein the "crucifixion is the main part of the meal...The cross is the table of the Lord where the bitter herbs and the pascal lamb are consumed" (Feeley-Harnik, 129). The author finds that the traditional four cups of wine, for example, are indeed represented in the larger scene of the Passion. The first cup occurs at the meal in question. The second cup is suggested in the Garden when Jesus asks that the cup be taken from him. The third cup is represented by that drink which Jesus is given at the crucifixion. The fourth, then, is that cup which must have been taken at the very end of the documents which portray the meals the resurrected Jesus shares with his disciples (cf. Luke 24:30f and 41f). This helps explain why a single cup would have been mentioned at a meal which was thought to be a seder. Perhaps it was the "literal" cup, meant to symbolize the Jews. The afikoman, which is a broken piece of matzah at the Seder hidden by the leader of the meal in order for the children to find after the meal, is Jesus himself! Lastly, Jesus has traditionally been regarded as the (Pascal) Lamb of God. Feeley-Harnik analyzes the entire Passion as an Haggadah narrative (cf. 129ff).

Feeley-Harnik's is a creative approach which deserves continual attention. I am curious, however, about how well the typological argument works. Initially, the argument seems odd in a text which both assumes Christianity to be true and says that the power of God is "manifested in his ability to control food" (72: from which it follows, as Feeley-Harnik states, that "to feed bad food or to starve is to judge or punish, to confer death"). We have a simple and compelling parallel which will be with us throughout: the goodness of God is equivalent to good food whereas punishment is equivalent to bad food.

If we stay with the analysis as it has been presented, we are confronted with a perspective of the crucifixion which is not adequately termed a "mystery." Rather, the crucifixion is "indigestible"; the occurrence of the death of Jesus was an event turned sour. Lest you think I am arguing on the basis of a metaphoric ambiguity, Feeley-Harnik herself says the Last Supper "was only the last in a long series of culinary disorders" (19). She refers to her assessment as a "shocking conclusion." Rather, we would say, it is "upsetting."

Feeley-Harnik finds several hitherto unmentioned parallels between the Exodus and the Passion. Just as the Seder was to be a feast at an appointed time (Exod. 12:6; 23:15), so did Jesus' death occur at the appointed time (cf. Matt. 26:1-2; Feeley-Harnik 130-31). As the Israelites left Egypt in haste (Exod. 12:11), so Jesus exhorts his disciples to be ready (cf. Matt. 24:43-44; Feeley-Harnik 130-31). Last, we may mention the author having found that the Bible commanded the Israelites to stay indoors on the eve of the Passover. Jesus and his company go outdoors where, "as if in fulfillment of the threat implied in the Exodus narrative, Jesus is not passed over. He is seized by his enemies" (133). We may ignore the question concerning the apparently safe going out of the Chief Priests.

The argument that Jesus having gone out of his quarters on the night of Passover would seem to indicate that the Last Supper was not a Seder (precisely because going ut would be a violation of a biblical command) is not cogent. The biblical narrative suggests death would be the result of going out during this night, and this is precisely what happened. An alternative would be to consider Jesus having gone outdoors in violation of the biblical injunction. But it is difficult to imagine Jesus testing the Bible on this issue. If Jesus had gone outside precisely in order to die, which some commentators may not be so eager to dismiss (for example, Schoenfeld), this would constitute an act of endangering one's life and would, therefore, also be a violation of the Bible. Again, we note that the mystery is removed from the fact of the death of Jesus. Yet the fact is still undigestible.

We can no longer term as typological exposition those interpretations which an author recites without coagulation by previous authors. Feeley-Harnik, I believe, makes several erroneous statements which are meant to be supportive of her thesis that Jesus' Passion was a universalization of the Passover. For example, Isaac has traditionally been regarded as an anti-type of Jesus. According to Christian theology, Jesus, as the correction of history, is the proper sacrifice of Isaac. Isaac in other words, had been an inadequate figure of Jesus. Feeley-Harnik goes too far when she states that "Isaac died in Jesus' passover...The union of Jews and Gentiles could be achieved only by destroying the relationship between fathers and sons" (141). It does not occur to our author that: (i) not only did Isaac not die, but the emphasis in Genesis is on multiplying and continuing life in spite of adversity (Gen. 22:17ff); (ii) that with his death Jesus was not passed over, was not spared affliction on the night of not going out; (iii) that the "union" Feeley-Harnik speaks of is based on the late death of one of the terms of relation; and (iv) the father/son relationship, if it is not irrelevant, seems promoted in the text of Genesis where the seed of the righteous man is deemed to be a blessing to his children. Not only does this seem to be poorly phrased theology, but is a bad metaphor.

Elsewhere our author states, "Despite appearances, union, rather than election, is the guarantee of eternal life" (149). This idea needs to be qualified. There was unity at the building of the tower of Babel, but the solidarity was neither blessed nor sanctified. Indeed, Genesis 49:6 bides one not to enter into unity with the angry. Hence, not only one's purpose, but one's attitude need to be considered before joint ventures may be undertaken. The prophets envisioned a kind of unity which may be termed "intranationalism." Isaiah, for example, states that when the Day of the Lord occurs, "Israel shall rank with Egypt and Assyria, those three, and there shall be a blessing in the center of the world" (Isa. 19:24). In that day, "all people may walk, each in the name they give God" (Mic. 4:5). The prophets view an era of peace, prosperity and plenty. They clearly indicate that separate nations will remain separate, and diverse cultures will continue in their distinction. What will change, we may surmise, is intolerance and the Hobbesian state of continual warfare, in mind and between bodies.

It would not seem to be "idealistic" or utopian for individuals and groups to begin living as if the divine era of intranationalism were within reach of the consequences of our intentions and considered actions. This requires courage. It necessitates understanding rather than contention. If so, the universalism of Jesus, as understood by the theologian, may be criticized for failing to be universal in a prophetic sense. Let us consider a specific example where intranationalism may be cogent. Metaphoric theology, such as that under consideration, may view the Jewish concern for Kashruth (dietary laws) as that practice which "severs Jews from Gentiles at every bite" (139). Jesus did not, as is clear, attempt to transform dietary laws into symbols of universal significance. But it is questionable whether the mission to the Gentiles was meant to bring Jews and Gentiles into ritualistic table fellowship with the community (as suggested in Acts 2:42ff) or was rather intended to obliterate the distinction "between eaten and uneaten, edible and inedible" (139). I submit that the latter is no longer typology, but akin to mysticism. Such logic leads to the making of morally atrocious comments such as, "Human sacrifice is superior to animal sacrifice as Jesus-Manna is superior to Moses-Manna" (ibid.). The prophets spoke against sacrifices in general, demanding human righteousness. I do not believe the prophets would have been opposed to the rabbinic notion that, at least since the destruction of the Temple, one's table manner becomes a sacrifice to God (cf. Baba Bathra 60b). Keeping Kosher, then, may be regarded as one way Jews reassert their -- particular to this culture -- devotion to the prophetic ideal. In this sense, to have once enjoyed lobster but to refrain is a method of keeping conscious of the requirements of God. If so, it is not an improved but simply a different culture which enjoins the eating of "all kinds of animals, clean and unclean, indiscriminately" in order to enact their devotion to God (162).

Jews themselves frequently submit to ritual observance with the consideration that such behavior is meant to keep them separate and distinct from non-Jews. Distinction certainly is a valorous quest. But if one performs only in order to be separate, one sets a precedent for reaching to extremism. Hence, the quest for distinction must be based on a "higher" principle. In order to expose the fallacy of the contrary notion, consider the following Mishna. Pe'ah 1:1 says the following are the things for which no definite qualities are prescribed; (i) leaving unreaped portions of the field for the poor and strangers, (ii) the gathering of the first fruits presented to the priests, (iii) the offering brought to the Lord during the pilgrimage festivals, (iv) the practice of loving-kindness, and (v) study of Torah. The fact that, unlike other requirements, no upper limit is given to the worshiper indicates that these five obligations are among the most important to Judaism. It is interesting, then, that the first three deal with events surrounding our table-fellowship, or at least fulfilling the biblical necessity of keeping certain sections of the religious relationship fed. It is notable that the five are given in what must be construed as an ascending order of importance. An argument that Torah study was paramount in Judaism would be superfluous. Torah is said to outweigh all sacrifices (Menahot 110a) and even an idol worshiper who is occupied with Torah is likened to the high Priest (Baba Kamma 38a). Nevertheless, the beginning and end of Torah is the performance of deeds of loving-kindness (Sotah 14a), as Hillel taught, "What is hateful to you, do not do to your fellow. That is the whole Torah; the rest is commentary. Now, go and learn" (Shabbat 31a). And what does one learn? How to perform deeds of loving-kindness! These included service to God as well as to one's fellow. As suggested above, one manner in which service to God occurs, at least since the destruction of the Temple, is through table fellowship (of which Passover is an example having developed from a pilgrimage festival).

As a final consideration, the three deeds under discussion have a correspondence with the three things upon which, according to Simon the Righteous, the world is based. As mentioned in Aboth 1:2, these are Torah, divine service, and the practice of loving-kindness. If the importance of these three requirements is granted, the following facts become evident: First, food related worship is only a portion of religious service, and not the most significant. Second, the higher aspects of food related services are not necessarily concerned with consumption, but offerings to God, food left behind, or food given away. If so, it is not the case that keeping a kosher kitchen is restrictive on the performance of righteous actions. Nor, it may be added, is it the case that refusal to keep kosher is more convivial to universalization.

This discussion serves to point out that Christianity did not, as Feeley-Harnik asserts, "transform the law by means of a process of interpretation known as midrash" (18). It is rather the case that the law, or in this instance the dietary law, was rejected outright. As noted above, Feeley-Harnik's text is best understood as a typological exegesis, not midrash. There are some important differences between the two methods of interpretation which need to be noted.

Typology focuses on the single event of Jesus' Passion, death and resurrection. Every prior event in history or thought either falls under this singular perspective, or else is rejected. Midrash, on the other hand, proceeds by conquering every singular event or idea until it yields a plethora of information and suggestions. Midrash does not bid one to accept the dogma of symbols. Indeed the very nature of drawing forth an abundance of ideas and implications precludes concentration on a terminal symbol. Insofar as typology proceeds by determining how a specific item of written (prior) text fits into an already decisive contemporary truth, typology is the elevation of pre-judgements. Midrash, on the contrary, is an elevation of the process of continual exegesis and commentary. Typology relies on the supposed ultimate end of experience whereas Midrash draws from the bottomlessness of Torah (cf. Job 11:9). It is as if the truth which is eternal is a truth which can only be perceived through repeated approximations. The infinite meaningfulness of life is barely understood unless all avenues of approach are utilized. Knowledge proceeds not only through reason, but through intuition as well; not only through precise discourse, but together with experimentation.

Neither Midrash nor typology are particularly concerned with the overall context of a biblical passage. Each is ultimately concerned to make the Bible more contemporary with the particular perspective of the author of an observation. Midrash accomplishes this by creative transformation of any given passage in order to read out every sense which may possibly be implied in the portion. Jews are instructed to inspect the literature repeatedly because "everything is in there" (Aboth 5:22). Typology, on the other hand, proceeds by applying every verse which became of interest in relationship to Jesus. Was Moses a law-giver? He only pre-figured the perfect law dispensed by Jesus. If Noah's ark was constructed of wood, it was but a symbol of the Cross. We have noted how the sacrifice of Isaac was treated. In sum, we may say that whereas Midrashim are extensive, typology is intensive.

Feeley-Harnik says that most of the time Jesus' disciples "do not understand what he is saying unless he finally speaks to them in food" (167). In terms of her own theology, Jesus is not understood until his Passion is regarded as a Passover. If this is the case, Feeley-Harnik is mistaken. The Seder is not an anti-type of Jesus' Passion (however coherent the Christian story may be approached as an abstraction of the Exodus story). Certainly there are resemblances, as there are between any phenomena which are placed in competition. It will be enough to note, in conclusion, that Christianity did not break from the kitchen of Judaism until the message of Jesus' resurrection was promulgated throughout Judea, Samaria and even to the ends of the earth (Acts 1:8).

I submit it was the assertion of Jesus having been resurrected (hence proving there was more than this earthly existence) which attracted converts to Christianity instead of Judaism. It was not the presence of a ritual table, nor the supposed restrictions of distinct dishes. What attracted people was the message, first, that Jesus had become like a heavenly being and, second, that he was able to pull his friends through to the other side. Food was not an issue, and typology was a remote consideration. This was made clear in Jesus' answer to the Sadducee that, at the resurrection, men and women do not engage in carnal behavior, such as eating and drinking, but become like the angels in heaven (Matt. 22:30). The story of Jesus is not the confection of the Seder, whatever their similarities. It is the threat of the end of this distinct celebration. This is the most important lesson we might learn from The Lords Table. Feeley-Harnik began by asking if the Last Supper was a Seder. She ended by dissolving the Jewish meal. She did not digest it.

Chapter Four

Jewish-Christian Relations and the Thought of Samuel Sandmel

Samuel Sandmel was a rare human being. He was a scholar, but his writings were relatively popular; he was intelligent, yet his works are clear, and readable. One text in particular, Two Living Traditions: Essays on Religion and the Bible, deserves attention as probably the best collection of his essays on topics as diverse as the Rabbinic enterprise, Jesus, and the Bible which is common to our religious and cultural heritage.

The following is not a review of Sandmel's work, but an attempt to vault the question which asks why a Jew should be interested in the figure of Jesus. At one point, Sandmel says that Jews who deals with this subject exhibit "the acme of delicacy" (17), and points out that his own contributions of expression about Jesus are "quantitatively the least among those who have written in this area" (18). Nevertheless, Sandmel's authorship on cognate issues is, as the text at hand indicates, diverse.

Sandmel says the Christian documents "give a mixture of reliable and unreliable history, but we do not know any responsible method to separate the strands from each other" (188; written ca. 1966). With this statement Sandmel perhaps misrepresents himself. There may quite well be a principle which would allow us to separate the genuine utterances of Jesus from the spurious, the original from the additional. But this is not the issue. It is not what Jesus did or did not say, but what he was and is taken to have meant, and how a movement developed from its own understanding of Jesus. What is at issue, in other words, is the difference between Judaism and Christianity. It is interesting to speculate how the two paths came to be separate, how they can have accepted so much common tradition and ideology, and then to have moved into diverse orbits of concern and interest.

There is nothing erroneous about diverse interpretations. The revitalization and contemporization of tradition is necessary and of positive value. Further, there is no *a priori* reason which makes it axiomatic that the "original" was better. It is just earlier. Finally, from what we do know about the earliest followers of Jesus, their form of respect for their master was not the same as the tradition which became dominant. What we assume to be the most historical and least historical, and all versions in-between, are various formulations which aid our understanding of, not Jesus, but the community which professed knowledge about him. It is interesting to note that Jesus had little or no universal significance apart from his earliest followers, no world-historical importance until the disciples and Paul emphasized their communal belief. This does not, however, bring us any closer to understanding contemporary positions.

Yet it seems discussion between Jews and Christians either begins with historical issues, or at least necessarily includes them in the dialogue. This is not to be lamented. If discussion does nothing else, if debate over what truly was or was not does not lead to conclusions, it at least puts us into a region where reason is called upon and sensitivity is demanded. I assume that, aside from interpretations, historical facts can be determined and distinguished from assertions which were not factual. We can agree, in other words, on some facts, and we allow that other claims are from another realm: belief. Neither community speaks disparagingly of belief, nor should (or can) they.

In general, Jewish authors are indeed in a delicate position when they write about Jesus. I think it fair to say that their position is paradoxical. While knowing the Christian claims for Jesus, Jews deny these claims, put forth arguments to show why these claims cannot be true, and yet honestly think they do not mean to disillusion the Christian believer. It is as if one says: "You are wrong, reason and evidence prove you are wrong, here are the reasons and the proof, but I am not out to deny or change you."

By the same token, the Jew who writes about Jesus generally has no ax to grind. Unless he or she is writing to a particular segment of the Jewish community willing to accept "irrational" beliefs, or erroneous ideas --and I trust we Jews to do not contribute to these ranks in any large number on most issues -- the Jew is not out to revile Jesus, nor "correct" Christianity, nor to offer his or her private version of "truth." Every Jewish author who would undertake to essay Jesus and the Judaisms of his day will have studied both Bible, non-canonical literature, and Talmud and Midrashim (Rabbinic traditions). If so, however, he or she will know there is no single correct interpretation, no immutable truth except one -- God -- who will do as He/She, pleases without human permission or aid. Thus, approach to questions about Jesus are a matter of curiosity. This curiosity, however, knits into contemporary issues.

In addition to the distinction between "original" and "interpretative," where neither ought to be called superior without further argument, we might mention the Jewish works on Jesus which compare and contrast Judaism and Christianity. This may occur through comparing and contrasting, for example, Jesus and Akiba, or Jesus and Rabbi Eliezer. These works may indicate how we are similar (few contemporary texts argue for superiority). Our various communities are in some ways the same and in some different; but this is no indication of what is better or what is worse. Indeed, it seems to be the case that one community performs as it does because that way is better for that particular community. The alternative is performance out of mere habit, but habituated communities are on the verge of death. Luckily, much of Judaism and much of Christianity are still creative. Further, it seems historically the case that when stagnation seems to threaten either community, thinkers arise who revitalize the faith.

The delicate position of the Jews ought not be an inhibition to speaking honestly and candidly. The fear of offending will merely leave us at a fork in the road. One advocate argues we ought not speak about Jesus at all. In this manner, or so the argument goes, we can prevent hurt feelings. However, for a scholar to keep silent seems a greater offense than genuine inquiry into sensitive issues.

A second advocate advises we totally view Jesus in Jewish belief structures. Two points may be raise against this perspective. First, if Jesus were so thoroughly what we today mean by a Jew, we have no grounds for understanding, or even assuming, the rise of Christianity. There must have been some differences of opinion between Jesus and the rabbis, even if the reports in the documents are exaggerated. There must have been something Jesus offered his followers which the Judaisms of the time did not. Nor do I mean to suggest that Jesus was not a Jew. Clearly he was, as his defense of the temple indicates, as his bold acceptance of the prophetic critique indicates. A related point is that the Judaisms of Jesus' time were not as unified as is too easy to believe. Judaism was probably a lot like the condition of the Jews, or the State of Israel is today, with major factions and minor parties spanning from ultra-liberalism to neo-conservatism. Indeed, given the Sadducean Priests, the Essenes, the Zealots, the Apocalyptical school, and the Pharisees, who themselves were divided into at least two distinct schools of thought (the progressives and the conservatives, the schools of Hillel and Shammai), and who knows how many other splinter groups, the effort to completely submerge Jesus into Judaism must become a ridiculously inappropriate chore. It raises more questions than can be answered.

A different position so completely severs Christianity from its creative development atop Jewish roots -- those tangled tendons of agreement and disagreement -- that we are left without any base of communication. How can we engage in a dialogue with a community which has absolutely nothing in common with us, even that which they claim to be primary and essential? Foreign as claims about Jesus from Christian theologians may seem to a Jew, as a matter of authentic Christian thought, theology ought to be dealt with at least on its own terms.

The Jew does not stand in relation to Jesus as the Christian stands in relation to Moses. Nor is it a stand-off. Moses is a necessary predecessor to Jesus in Christian ideology. But Jesus does not stand in any essential relationship with Judaism. Jesus neither contributed to Judaism as an ongoing and developing response to life nor did he add to Jewish history. Nor did Jesus negate Jewish life, as Marx and Spinoza. Nor did Jesus subtract from the store of Jewish knowledge and wisdom. The Jew stands in relation to Jesus as the Christian may stand in relation to the Buddha. He is a figure in world history. The Kierkegaardian paradox from the Jewish perspective is that a loyal son of Israel became a force of opposition, and remains both at one and the same time.

It is true, as suggested above, that faith is largely subjective and cannot be harmed by scholarly or scientific study. Indeed, science and scholarship should supplement faith: for no true commitment to God can be based on dishonesty or illusion. While it may be true that nearly every belief begins with "irrational, unsupportable" (historically impossible) events -- the burning bush, the transfiguration, the angel who appeared to Mohammed -- each community of belief develops to a point at which they act as if they decided to base their truths on reason instead of miracle. For Judaism, this reliance on reason is apparent in the Talmudic literature; with Christianity in the halls of the scholastics. We Jews have a saying: From Moses (of the burning bush) to Moses (of the rationalistic Guide For the Perplexed), there is none like Moses. It is not immediately clear to which Moses the saying refers. Apparently, we Jews are given the choice -- the span -- from miracles and faith to logic and reason. Judaism involves both. Others suggest the second Moses is Mendelssohn, the German Philosopher. Oddly enough, this does not complicate the issue.

I suggest we Jews and Christians meet on the grounds of reasoned inquiry. The investigations of Jews into the historical Jesus ought no more be offensive than the theologians inquiry into the "Christ of faith." Yet each ought to be undertaken with good faith; honesty, critical acumen, and with an eye toward understanding more creativity.

Jews ought to overcome any residual traces of the idea that speaking about Jesus is completely unrelated to the "Jewish" realm of inquiry. Formerly, the treatment of Jewish subjects was thought to be limited to study of the proper mode of sacrifice, determining when a ritual bath was required, and the procedure to be followed on citing a new moon. These are still important areas of study and concern. Nor do we ignore "scholarly" studies: mysticism, socio-political analyses, philosophy, etc.

The figure of Jesus ought to be as much a part of our discourse as any other aspect of Jewish history. If we study the debates the Rabbis had with the priestly authorities in the Temple, we can with as much justification study the earliest followers of Jesus. If we study the relation of the Ten Martyrs with the government of Rome, we can with as much justification study our own relation with the peoples among whom we live. There is even more justification to do so inasmuch as understanding contemporary situations and events is at least as importance as understanding those long past.

The Jew who writes about Jesus or Christianity is not usurping sacred domain. At the very least, the Jew can contribute a distinct perspective with which both Jews and Christians can compare and contrast their own beliefs. This is important not primarily because of what the Jew may say, but for the challenge to become clear on issues too often taken for granted, to think about ideas which would never otherwise have been raised.

Sandmel gave two reasons for his study of Jesus or Christianity. Since Jews no longer live in the ghetto, are no longer insulated "from the stream of Western thought, Jesus and Christianity inevitably swim into our kin, and therefore our participation in Western culture implies a need to encounter all of its facts" (19f). Secondly, Sandmel says, "scholarship is at best when it is as broad as possible," and study of these issues is not only relevant to the Second Commonwealth period, but "it is illegitimate" for the Jewish scholar of that period, or any other, not to investigate all the phenomena of the time (19). In fact, rabbinic Judaism first began to come into its own about the time Christianity was being formed and fermented. To understand our own contemporary Judaism, we ought to understand how and why a different form derived from the same conditions. Why have the Essenes disappeared? Why are the Sadducees no more? What happened to the Apocalyptic sects? Further, we ought to ask why only two out of untold numbers survived. If Sandmel is correct, then, extensive scholarship is necessary not only for understanding the world in which we live, but for understanding ourselves as well.

Yet Sandmel implies a third reason in a different context. Interpreting Philo's de Decalogo as a utilization of Stoic rhetoric to defend Jewish revelation, Sandmel ends on what almost seems a plea that this were not what Philo was doing. "How good it would have been had Philo argued that Jewish ethics was different even in substance from the Stoic, and prove it! How good it would be if we could contend that Jewish ethics surpasses the secular, *and prove it*!" (290 - emphasis added). Sandmel does not here recommend we do something different than calm, detached and objective analyses, but suggests the benefit of perceiving the differences between perspectives and asserting these differences. I assume that Sandmel would allow the Stoic a similar task. What he recommends is not propaganda and persuasion, but propagation of principles. Clear presentation of our terms in debate with alternative arguments will change neither our positions nor that of the other, but should aid in clarifying our own position, and help develop our mutual wisdom.

We are different and distinct, but nevertheless human beings. We have different behaviors, and believe different statements. By and large, however, Jews and Christians assert they have a similar obligation to their fellow human being. The much more beneficial and necessary ties of moral obligation and ethical development ought to be given primary consideration.

Finally, students of Jesus and Christianity can help a Jew clarify an internally Jewish issue. If early Christianity was "a Jewish movement which was in particular ways distinctive from other Judaisms" (294), study of the reasons Judaism and Christianity developed in diverse directions will take us a long way towards answering the question which asks "What is a Jew?"

Sandmel had written that to "see the way in which Christians treat the issue of law and non-law can broaden the perspectives of the modern Jewish theologian" (57). Similar benefits accrue when Christian theologians view the treatment of repentance and forgiveness, or related issues from the Jewish perspective. Again, it is not a question of superiority, but different responses to universal human needs. Sandmel went on to say that "to transfer into Judaism even the overtone of the antithesis [between law and grace] can result only in distorting the nature of Judaism" (ibid). The issue is clearly not to allow the other to interpret our faith community, but to allow the other to speak openly and critically from his or her faith community, and for us to learn from his or her comments or criticisms. This requires we advance dialogue beyond mere tactfulness.

To give an example, Sandmel says that "in the Christian approach providence is dominant and free will is recessive, while in Judaism free will is dominant and providence recessive" (60). Discussion is not meant to resolve the issue, but to speak about our communities to one another. An additional advantage will be to present the very issues of free will and providence to our laity. What is interesting is the apparent fact that the terms of discussion were similar ever since the beginning. At one point, the participants in dialogue between the disciples of the sages and the followers of Jesus must have had some interesting and enlightening discussions. Still, Judaism survived and Christianity survived. Understanding why they are different is as important as why they are similar. The scientific side of scholarship is not in competition with different faiths.

We speak toward the day when scientific inquiry and sympathetic lifestyles are also the two sides of faith. Sandmel has taken us quite a way up this road.

Chapter 5

Confrontation or Conversation: Models for Jewish-Christian Dialogue

The Distinction Presented

Confrontational interpretation is a popular form of argument among both Jews and Christians. Simply stated, confrontational interpretation is a methodological form of argument which assumes both that there are issues which must be resolved and, ironically, that resolution (or clarification) will resemble the position of the exponent. Every available rhetorical tool is utilized to prove that there are not two sides to each issue, and that when two sides appear, one side is in error.

Criticism of confrontational interpretation assumes the following principle (which may need to be proved): methodology determines perspective. The structure of the ways in which we think are the limits (however narrow or wide) of what we think. It remains true that insights attained "around our limitation," as it were, may contribute to a piecemeal modification of our method, but methods entirely structure our thoughts. Methodology determines the questions we ask, the direction we take in order to achieve an answer and, because both the general method and the form of argument are limitations to the answer we derive, the content as well. Any particular method of interpretation, then, is the premise of the limits of that which may be stated.

In contrast to confrontational methodology is the conversational style. We need no special characterization of this type of speech. The term 'conversational' designates how people speak without defenses, without barriers. Conversation has no planned structure. When we are speaking with one another, we are continually present to that which may startle. One never knows what may be said by the person with whom one is speaking. Insights are more readily available to those who engage in conversation, even if it remains true that the insights produced are subject to revision or classification in order to be presented in a suitable sense. One often hears, in a conversation, "That is an interesting suggestion" or "I will have to think about that." One rarely hears such remarks in a debate. Rather, one hears: "Your remark is not cogent, does not fit the facts," and so on. Conversational style is not combative, and is confrontational only in the sense of being there with the other person.

Richard Rorty defines "culture as conversation" (Rorty 319) wherein the point is "to keep the conversation going rather than to find objective truth" (377). Rorty draws the deeper moral of the contrast with which we are concerned by implying that evasion of the assessment of true and false is proper. Rorty says that what is important is that disagreeing partners are agreeable to the prevention of hunger, or building a world where there is no need for a secret police (388-89).

The difference between formal argument, which I claim is confrontational, and informal discussion, which makes allowances for claims or ideas not completely submerged in a methodological presentation, may be applied to dialogues or ecumenical discussions. Formal arguments always have a point to prove. If this attitude is taken into ecumenical situations, one is not available to hear about differences between groups which may erroneously be thought debilitating. In this manner, the erroneous impression of structural defects is not put aside. Rather, the situation becomes a registry of differences which are aligned as various sides of an issue. As we saw above, once sides are determined there is an effort to prove one side right and the other wrong. Yet dialogues are not primarily for purposes of determination of issues. It follows that they are not arenas for proving points. While it is true that each participant may have his or her own insights and impressions to convey, the first principle of discussion is to understand. The participant, therefore, must be able to put aside his or her desire to utter proof. This does not mean the participant must disown his or her knowledge of truth. As little as one can leave behind one's physical features can even a momentary forsaking of beliefs occur. This is neither possible nor required. Nor would the act of bracketing one's beliefs allow one to contribute to the needs of the moment.

The promotion of human understanding cannot be based on antagonistic contrasts. The enhancement and advancement of appreciation and cooperation between Christians and Jews is one of the more valuable endeavors today. We cannot, then, risk dealing with issues of magnitude in terms which are similar to those used in the disputations and polemics of yesterday. Discussions based on conflict, on half-presentation of truth, too summarily dismisses common terms, and does not deserve the name "discussion."

If it is the case that neither a confrontational pose necessitating resolution of issues nor an attitude of disinterest is suitable, a methodology must be discovered which is at one and the same time non-confrontational yet not so casual as to allow our separate interests and ideas to be negated. An additional benefit will accrue if the proposed method allows the insights which are potentially available in conversation to be developed into the structure of conversation. In the remarks which follow, I hope to show that narrative theology offers precisely such a method. My burden is to accomplish this task in a non-confrontational manner. While this will leave my arguments necessarily abstract, I trust I will leave an impression of what is necessary in intra-religious dialogues. I do not violate the self-imposed limitations of my treatment of the subject if I confront a particular method of argument and offer narrative theology as a cogent alternative.

The Dialectical Paradigm

Dialectical arguments may be taken as a paradigm of the confrontational method. In fact, by using the term "argument" I have limited the traditional function of what has been known, in the West at least, as dialectics. The term is as ambiguous as anyone may wish. A context is needed in order to make sense of what is meant by the term "dialectics." Although originally denoting the thinking of two things together, dialectics may refer to one or more of the following: (i) any process of movement from one set of circumstances (S1) to another set of circumstances (S2); (ii) a particular process of movement from S1 to S2; (iii) any condition of reciprocal tension thought to necessitate (or be identifiable in the sense of) working itself out in terms of S1 to S2; (iv) a particular series of arguments analyzing or projecting movement from S1 to S2; (v) the particular system of analysis associated with the name of Hegel, or Marx, or any of several other "dialecticians"; (vi) a particular analysis of a particular movement from S1 to S2 offered by any of the above authors. Each of these particular identifications of a dialectic and (if this method is paradigmatic of all confrontational methods) every other method initiates analysis with the premise of a statement (or fact) and presents logical, empirical, or otherwise nullifying contradictions to the initial statement (or fact). A particular instance will show the inadequacy of the method.

The standard assumption among people with inadequate knowledge holds that the God of the "Old Testament" is vengeful whereas the God of the New is loving. This has certainly not been the case in every investigation of the Hebrew Scriptures, but has been popular enough to merit discussion. The statement as it stands clearly does not suggest, as may be obvious, that people approach the issue of God's being with different, more or less adequate perspectives. Rather does this notion suggest that there are two Gods: a vengeful God and a loving God. The idea of two gods, the first having authored the legalistic texts and the latter having inspired the agape texts, may have been suggested to "the first theologians" by the gnostic emphasis in developing Christianity (Lowry 95, *passim*). While structuring deep contrasts may be thought necessary for certain kinds of arguments, the suggestion that there are two gods can only be regarded as unacceptable to both Christians and Jews.

Michael Goldberg refers to Jews and Christians venerating "a different god altogether" (Goldberg, 1985, 218). Yet this decision is not the result of Jewish and Christian narrative. The literature of both Jews and Christians speak of the Holy One, the Creator and Master of the Universe. The diverse narratives presented in several stories, each with diverse emphasis, are in effect non-contradictory. An underlying current of interpretation (explicitly stated in those Jewish writings containing the exegetical methodology called "Midrash") explains that the results of previous studies of "the way" are not to be taken literally. "The way" is a term common to the earliest mention of Christian worship and Jewish halacha. As this may suggest, the way denotes a means of travel, not an announcement of arrival. The way, in other words, is the collection of our stories and rituals, prayers and creative ventures. Judaism and Christianity are, then, the "programs" of how

Jews and how Christians have, and currently do, behave in their sincere quest to live the good life.

The term "program" may suggest both traditional perspectives of how things were done within each community as well as the (often implicit) statement of the direction each community expects to take. This second suggestion deserves attention. Both Jews and Christians have broad ranging political programs to guide their journey through the world as well as statements of what is necessary in order to assure survival of the soul, or spirit, or some other faculty, after leaving the world. In the definitive hermeneutic of each religion, these mortal and spiritual perspectives must each be coherent in terms of each other. One cannot, to take an obvious example, commit robbery and at the same time assume one is a "good Jew" or "good Christian." It is the responsibility of each community to explain to its practitioners why the contrary assumption would be erroneous. I assume each community performs this task fairly well. The only reason the issue deserves mention is to insure that the coherent political/spiritual concerns of both Jews and Christians are not accounted as the fictitious Protocols of the Elders of Zion, a Catholic conspiracy to control the world, or any of a number of paranoid plans. Every community has political programs, but they are cogent largely in terms of aiding the community to survive (and possible contribute to the survival of others) until "the kingdom comes."

This discussion also serves to point out that while the traditions of Jews and Christians are certainly not identical, and the belief structures are not similar, the projective "programs" are often comparable. What Christians call "love" Jews call "loving-kindness." It would be interesting and beneficial to see more monographs devoted to investigating the use of different terms although the concepts are comprehended in terms of similar semantic structuring. The fact that more of these type studies are not undertaken is due to the continuing history and hermeneutic of conflict.

If we are not to take the previous analyses of our respective religions as literally true, how are we to hold onto them? In other words, if we are mandated to regard prior interpretation as relatively inadequate constructions, what is the point in continually seeking the adequate kernel within? We may reverse the suggestion contained in this question and say that every interpretation is (or should be) adequate for its time, yet every subsequent interpretation is (or should be) a closer approximation of the truth, or a more adequate presentation of the truth. The history of exegesis and criticism is, after all, long and progressive. It seems to be the case that even revelation, or especially revelation, requires continual analyses before clarity is achieved.

In spite of the suggestion that each traditional phase of interpretation may be retained as an ingredient in the subsequent approximation, there are some presentations which do not deserve to be retained. I began with a presentation of Goldberg's "phenomenological" analysis of conflicting perceptions of God being assumed to denote an ontological division in the Deity. His statement serves as an adequate introduction to confrontational interpretation inasmuch as certain theologians have held similar views. Pascal, for example, makes a distinction between the Jewish perspective or approximation of God and his own Christian perspective. We need not be detained by the fact that his "political" program against the Jesuits must ultimately suggest a concept of the deity which was different than theirs as well. This would only mean, as should be obvious, that there are several more or less adequate images of God among both Jews and Christians. Pascal willingly waived the numerous and subtle approximations of God as he concentrated on what was assumed to be the two predominant ones. "The Jews had a doctrine of God, as we have one of Christ" (Pascal 291). My thesis that confrontational analyses require division into categories, one good and one bad, is confirmed in Pascal's thought: "Either Jews or Christians must be wicked"" (Pascal 56). Pascal goes further by making the differences between Jews and Christians contribute to their eventual destiny: "There is no redeemer for the Jews...only for the Christians is there a redeemer" (Pascal 100).

It is not my intention to single out Pascal as an example of confrontational interpretation. Father Edward H. Flannery spoke of a continuing crescendo of Christian theological [read: methodological] perception of the Jews. My analysis suggests that malicious wickedness was not the guiding thread in this presentation of the Jews. What was decisive was the supposition of the necessity for an antithesis of the ideal Christian. St. Chrysostom called the Jews "lustful, rapacious, greedy, perfidious bandits" and other terms which served to present the Jew as "impure and impious" (quoted in Flannery 48). Father Flannery suggested St. Chrysostom was not an anti-Semite, but what is missing from Flannery's account is a justification for his defense of St. Chrysostom's good intentions. Mitigating circumstances are suggested by the need of contrasts demanded in conflicting accounts. If one is to be regarded as pure and pious, there must be another one which can be pointed toward as impure and impious. St. Chrysostom was not simply Jew-baiting if he were following the tradition of confrontational analyses. This does not excuse his having readily submitted to the convenience of contrast, but it does serve to explain his position.

I need not adduce quotes to show that the God of the Hebrew Bible was thought to be a God of mercy, a trustworthy contractor, and a faithful paternal/maternal figure. Nor need quotes be presented from the Christian Bible to show that God from the perspective of love did not give carte blanche for any and every behavior human beings may have devised. The Jewish and the Christian perspective of God each speak of a God who both promises and requires. While it may be the case that the promises are different, and the requirements are not identical, it is not the case that two gods are the objects of Jewish and Christian worship, devotion, and prayer. We end up thinking we are further apart than we really are when we paint broad outlines without portraying the historical developments, rhetorical nuances or critical apperceptions which follow upon any methodological structure. The broad outlines paint the canvas into sides which divide. The nuances and conversational insights which may be present to Jews or Christians "around the back of" their hermeneutic, as it were -- insights which may not find their way into the textbooks or doctrine for a generation or more -- not only fill out the sketch, but abolishes the need for the broad strokes of division.

I have argued that recognition of similarity beyond antagonistic contrasts will lead to a realistic approach to the contemporary concerns of dialogue and intra-religious relationship. This casual approach to the issues of Jewish-Christian discussions, addressing the topics from the perspective of our concern for agreement in order to fill in the background with particular distinctions rather than beginning with the contrasts in order to maintain lines of division, has the further benefit of allowing recognition of developments and trajectories which are neither biblical nor necessarily normative. Unassimilated insights may yet be acceptable.

Syntheses and Resolutions

It is not the case that the meeting of Jews and Christians is meant to resolve itself into a "synthesis." This is neither expected nor desired by either community. The different communities do not confront one another as opposites needing resolution. Although there may be a certain tension between Jews and Christians, the tension may be relieved in conversation. Relief is not resolution. Whereas resolution occurs after a confrontational debate, in which there are winners and losers, relief comes with understanding. We may assume that Jews and Christians face one another not to negate their own positions, but rather to contribute to their allegiance, the alliance of communities seeking understanding in order to better serve God.

If the word "synthesis" is used in this context, it can only refer to the continual development of understanding between Jews and Christians. But we already possess a perfectly good term to designate this contemporary involvement: conversation. In dialogue, Jews will not become Christians, nor will Christians become Jews. If this would occur it would be a great deformity. We ought rather enjoy diversity and the opportunity offered for alternative presentations of approximation of that which is true. In retrospect, the too often too silent dialogue between Christians and Jews is seen not to be opposition, but merely tension. Understanding contains the implicit premise that we search in order to recognize both the similarity and divergence between separate communities (and even within communities). We ought also study the whys and wherefores of the differences and similarities. As corporate entities, both Jews and Christians are beyond the tension of oppositional development, which is the hallmark of confrontational interpretation as well as the functional term which makes dialectics the paradigm of theological method. Defining one's own group in contrast to another group -- whether as a presentational dialectic of how the differences have emerged, or as the projection of how confrontation will lead to an ultimate truth -- is the white elephant of theology and scholarship.

The religious relationship, grasping some aspect of the eternal, resists or is beyond mediation in a dialectic. This is not to say that religious beings do not need the mediation of indicators. The creative tension of being together is necessarily contrasted with the destructive tension which demands an abolishing synthesis. Rejection of the notion of "synthesizing" all the terms contributing to dialogue into a resolve does not mean that we must give up the quest for our own creative advancement. It may be the case that the more alternatives which contribute to the "conglomerate" of facticity (i.e. the multi-dimensional or parallel lines which should be analyzed as contributing to the phenomenological construction or intention of what is otherwise too vacuously determined to be a "thesis" or "anti-thesis") the easier we may find living with difference. Everyone knows how eerie it is to walk down a long, dark street alone. Tension may be eased if even a relatively familiar stranger is on the same road. Tension is eased in an inverse relationship to the number of people on the same road. The more people (unless, of course, they form into a hostile group), the less tension. The same may be true in the social realm, or in the pluralistic structure demanded by discussion groups.

By Way of Conclusion

Although I have not talked about particular stories in the literature, it should be apparent how dialectics contrasts with narrative. Although dialectics may be understood in various forms, the fundamental form dialectics assumes in contemporary society is that of projection of resolutions to conflicts. Largely under the influence of Marx (who was under the influence of both Hegel, the idealist, and Darwin, the naturalist) dialectics in contemporary methodology is not the thinking of two things together but thinking them apart. Two other major trajectories of dialectics may be discounted: dialectics as a method of analyzing supposed manners of development and, alternatively, a method of speaking about perceptions of how things are (in tension).

Stories, by contrast, exist to be shared. In the social realm, the sharing of stories may be a method of relief from tension: stories explain, enhance, suggest, command, berate, soothe, and project. But they do so in a non-confrontational manner. This is because, by and large, one is free to understand a story on the level at which he or she is best able to approximate the lessons of the narrative. The manner of reception is dependent upon the hearer of the story. We hear in a context, that is true; but a good story is one which explains the context. Dialectics is supposed to *be* the context. Stories *support* the transcendent realm. Dialectics erroneously thinks it *is* the transcendent.

Gregory Bateson has proposed a useful distinction. In the material universe, which may be taken as the model for the dialectical model of confrontation, the cause of an event "is some force or impact exerted upon some part of the material system by some one other part" (Bateson 106). This suggests an image of clashing, random atoms. Bateson's statement certainly implies, in our context, that for every action there is an equal, if opposite, reaction. Hence, confrontation on one side requires confrontation on the other. The "natural" model, then, involves random clashing and possible violence. Bateson contrasted this with the non-material world, of which conversation and dialogue must be considered a single sub-category. "[I]t takes a relationship...to activate some third component" (ibid.). What this third component is we are not told. It would seem to depend upon the context of the relationship (the context created by the relationship).

Narrative is the formal way in which Jews and Christians make conversation among themselves. Homiletics, midrash, sermons, texts, speeches, and all forms of narration represent one Jew speaking to another, or one Christian speaking to another. If Elie Wiesel is correct when he says God loves stories, narrative is also one way in which people speak to God. I suggest narrative be investigated as a non-confrontational way of Jews speaking to Christians and Christians speaking to Jews.

Note

Jacob Neusner (1993) accomplished precisely that which was recommended at the conclusion of this paper. Neusner says we ought to abandon what Martin Heidegger called "calculative [manipulative] thinking" with regard to the other, and teach from the treasury of our separate traditions that which will shape our imaginations to elicit our sympathy for the (stories of the) other. The beginning of dialogue occurs in the realm of feeling, and our attitude toward the alien other. The first step is to know how the other feels (106). To know how the other feels requires the development of a certain attitude. Perhaps we may most easily find such a "dialogic" attitude through the narrative stories of the other. Those stories are so like/unlike our own.

Chapter Six

Jews and Catholics Discussing Bible and Jesus

In the previous chapter, I argued that Jewish-Christian dialogue cannot efficaciously proceed in a conflictory, confrontational manner. Rather, I agree with Paul Van Buren (1980) that dialogue is best perceived as "conversation" between like-minded people, relating with one another to achieve congenial understanding of the differences which divide them. This characterization suggests that participants in interfaith discussions need to be sympathetic yet critical; secure in their own faith, yet accepting of faiths different from their own. These "contrary" terms of an agreement between partners in dialogue indicates why discussions between Jews and Christians may be difficult -- but not impossible.

Not long ago, just such a Jewish-Catholic dialogue was held between a local Catholic church and synagogue. Previous meetings had never proceeded much beyond polite exchanges. My wife, Gilda, insists to this day that the congregants of the church are too sophisticated and democratic to get into any really good debates. She is accustomed to dialogue with born-again Christians who, whatever else their virtues or faults, are always willing to argue their point with feeling. At our latest meeting, there were some significant differences form previous evenings.

At this meeting, described by both Rabbi and Priest as "getting to the guts of the issues," there was a notable tension. The discussion centered around five photocopied passages from the Christian Bible (see Appendices A-E). We looked at Luke 2:21, an account of the

45

circumcision of Jesus; Luke 2:41-47, describing the pilgrimage of
Jesus' family to Jerusalem, and his discussions with the sages; followed
by Matthew 6:9-13, "the Lord's prayer." The Rabbi explained how
each line of the prayer was compatible with similar expressions or
sentiments in Jewish writings. He noted that "only for reasons of
historical association" will Jews not recite the "Our Father." We then
looked at John 2:13-17 concerning Jesus' driving the money changers
from the Temple. The Priest referred to this text as a zealous example
of an author showing Jesus defending the Temple in accord with the
belief that "Jesus is the new Temple." The Rabbi commented that, like
all temples in the ancient world, the Jewish Temple was "to the purpose
of sacrifice," and because of the international character of the people
who came to the Temple, "money changers were required to exchange
foreign currency into the coin of the land" in order that religious Jews
could purchase the doves, or other animals, which would be sacrificed
according to Scripture. He further suggested that to have carried a live
animal for sacrifice from Athens, Crete, or elsewhere, would have
constituted cruelty to the animal.

Finally we discussed Acts 4:11-12, describing Jesus as the keystone
rejected by the builders. The Priest explained that although the passage
was an example of antisemitism,[1] it was "understandable in a text
written around the year after the Christians had been forced out of the
synagogues as heretics. The Acts were written, in other words, as
Christians were attempting to establish themselves as a separate and
distinct community. My rabbi said of the text: "I cannot make sense
of this passage from a Jewish perspective."

After discussing the passage, we divided into three groups of
between eight and ten people, with the request for an equal number of
Christians and Jews in each group. We were to discuss the texts and
then formulate opinions about the final passage -- but I jump ahead.

When the rabbi said that he did not understand what was going on
in the "faith statement" contained in Acts (4:11-12), he was, of course,
relying on a distinction between himself as a scholar and himself as a
Jew. The scholar in the rabbi, just as the scholar in the priest,
undoubtedly understood very well what was going on in the passage.
Scholarship in this sense is not primarily concerned with interpretation,
but with historical development, and is therefore sharply distinguished
from theology. I do not suggest our clergy are schizophrenic, but
suggest these are extreme terms of a dialectic. It seems clear that the
dialectic between history and interpretation is too often resolved in

terms of a fundamentalist rejection of history, a secularistic rejection of theology, or a relatively arbitrary decision to remain somewhere between the two extremes. None of these alternatives can be regarded as particularly appealing, nor deemed a good solution to the encountered problems.

The Priest had originally broached the distinction between historical issues and theological ones. He said that, among scholars, there are few generally held opinions concerning the historical Jesus. "We do not," he added "have historically accurate reporting as one would find in 'The New York Times.' He then commented that the apparent transformation of the restrained sentiment of the earliest texts preserved by the Church (composed out of oral traditions at about the time of the destruction of the Temple) into the militant anti-Judaic tract preserved under the name of John (composed around the year 90) is evidence of a growing "ideological antisemitism" and certainly not the word of God." The Priest suggested that these words put into the mouth of Jesus convey an accurate sense of the historical relationship between Jews struggling to survive the destruction of their sacred institution, and Christians struggling to survive an identity crisis. I thought that the text chosen to illustrate the growing rift between Synagogue and Church was ambiguous at best. Surely there were better examples of hatred of Jews which could have been distributed. I was curious why John 8:44-47 (see Appendix F) was not reproduced, nor the passages which recount the Jews supposed clamoring for Jesus' death. I concluded that this may have indicated a skirting of the issue on the part of the organizers of the meeting, or a failure to deal directly with the fundamental cause of Christian anti-Jewish sentiments: Jews as Christ-killers.

No one who spoke that evening gave any indication that he or she believed in the "believe-it-or-be-damned" God who seems more congenial to literalists or fundamentalists. One rather elderly Catholic woman did say that, as a child, she was taught the "believe-it" version of her faith. But she, correctly in my opinion, spoke of a maturing process, and a more intelligent and personal commitment to Catholicism, entailing a more subtle, less literal, more complex and yet more efficacious understanding of faith. However, to quality the Bible as merely "God-inspired," and therefore liable to be revised -- as this woman seemed to express -- would seem a caricature of God's word. The manner in which we understand statements mediated by people would seem to rely on defective, or limited, understanding. It may be the case that theological language, which is generally non-biblical, may be defended precisely on the basis of maturation, or ever increasing approximations of truth. Yet such a defence may seem to wrest "authorship" from God. In this sense, if theological language were appropriate for increasing sensitivity to the divine, then reading theology back into the biblical era would require that we regard Scripture as evidence of human beings seeking the unspoken word of God. The Bible would not be the absolute-absolute, which is beyond human comprehension, nor would it be the absolute-particularized, which would be incompatible with the absolute being of the deity. In the latter instance, the Bible would become merely one historical document among others. The Bible would seem to be salvaged from this fate if it were regarded as the particular seeking the divine. Thus, Scriptures are historical documents, but they hold a principle place insofar as they summarize and propel the generations which study them. Further, this perspective allows us to disregard seemingly prejudiced remarks as merely historical, and completely non-theological.

I realize that this idea virtually excludes God from consideration as the direct author of the text. We do, however, retain God as the object of the text. This perception takes God out of a (fundamentalist) concern for exactitude and places ultimate concern back in the context of our lives. You understand, of course, that neither the rabbi nor the priest may have agreed. Nevertheless, if theology is manipulative, if it summarizes and expresses historical concern with that which is beyond history, then we do not have an absolute message in the Bible. If we pick and choose what is to be regarded as the word of God, by what criterion would we choose that which we would retain? The potential for rejecting the message of the Bible is most extreme in the case of our picking and choosing.

Thus, assuming a methodology agreeable to both Jews and Christians, our Catholic host for the evening said: "Of course what the Bible says is true. But this does not necessarily give us insight into the factual occurrence of any particular event." Of course the Bible is true, "but what does it mean?" If the meaning of an event or passage is something we must derive by interpretive acts, if meaning is something we must today struggle with and answer to our communal satisfaction, then the facticity of the event is at best secondary. When philosophy, theology, or midrash are at work, historical questions are secondary. Did Moses literally trudge up the mountain to receive two engraved stones of commandments, and then wearily carry them down to the people? No; but the story is true. That is, the story does contain an important insight. The story does teach us something, does give us a worthy image to contemplate, does challenge us to say what the tale means to us, and so on. The meanings may be as diverse as the symbolic or speculative wisdoms which apply themselves to the task of interpretation. If so, perhaps I should modify my claim and say that the Bible as I understand it, as human search for the divine, is beneficial for those who have not found God, who do not perceive a personal God, or do not fathom a revelatory God. Such a conception would be, then, a "minimal perception," by which I mean the least on a scale of values available to people of conviction, or in a condition where convictions conflict with other convictions.

As the Priest concluded his statement of distinction between the historical deficiencies and the theological assertions, I raised the following question. "Can we consider the faith-statements presented in the Book of Acts, a book written in the 80's, as an accurate restatement of the types of statements a member of the Christian group would have made in the 30's, while still a member of the synagogue? And if we are to regard them as such, why did the supposed rousting of Christians from Jewish institutions by declaring them heretics only occur in the mid-80's?" The Father's reply was straightforward. First, he said, we do not know the types of faith-statements the earliest Christians would have made. History is unreliable. Nevertheless, the remarks of Christians in the 80's have been historically conditioned. The burden was on the Christian community to prove themselves progressive and to portray the Jewish community as static. Finally, the Priest said: "We believe they did make faith-statements very much like the ones we make today, only without the historically conditioned antisemitism. [see note 1]."

I ignored the implication that history is only considered inaccurate when it is a question of what does not fit one's own view. History was being treated as erroneous in consideration of the development or modification of theologies. At least, this was my initial impression until I asked a follow-up question: "Do you think there is any correlation between the original followers of Jesus in the 30's, and the faith-statements presented in the text of the 80's?" He answered confidently, "Of course. There had to have been." If so, then it seems history has negatory powers over theology. History is the precondition of theological insight. The Priest did not elaborate his answer, but it seems reasonable to expect that an influx of Gentiles into the movement as it passed through pagan environs would have brought "foreign" influence. Whereas a Jew might say that history conditions theology, a Christian may want to say that theology uses history as a vehicle towards new theological truths. In fact, it seems the potent question regarding the divergence between the Jesus of history and the Christological Christ is decided by the participants standing with regard to the impingement or service claimed for the dialectic between history and theology.

Before we can discuss the person and being of Jesus, the schism between the earliest followers of Jesus and the Jewish community must be addressed. A respectable theologian, Karl Rahner, referred to the parting of the ways as being achieved "with immense difficulties...[having become] a Church that entered into a dialogue with the times" (Rahner, 1968, 140). Rahner approves of such a dialogue "with the times," as is evident in his own association with Vatican II, but he emphasized that if this means "that therefore the Church must give in - that I cannot admit" (Rahner, 1968, 139).

I do not believe most Jews appreciate the difficulty with which the Jews who followed Jesus must have had in breaking with the community of Israel. There is evidence in the book of Acts and elsewhere which suggests the Palestinian Jews did not in fact break with the community. The apostle Paul, a Hellenist-Jew, and therefore tainted with Greek ideology and speculation, is largely regarded among Jews as the source of divergence between Judaism and the "Christian" members of the community. This is a common view in spite of the fact that Jews will be the first to assert that the Jewish community, before the destruction of the Temple, was eclectic and not at all monolithic.

On the Jewish side, the problem is inverse to the one I raised. If Jewish-Christians were good Jews, if they worshipped in synagogues and at the Temple until the Temple was destroyed,[2] and if they only began to leave the synagogues when the late curse on heretics was formulated, then the issue of their commitment is raised. If Jewish-Christians were recognized as "normative" Jews, acceptable by the Jewish community from the year 30 through the year 70 (which is an entire generation), what was it about Jesus which held him dear to the memory of those Jews? What kind of charisma can have spanned an entire generation and, indeed, these thousands of years? The easy answer, of course, is that the Hellenist Jews who were not tied to Jerusalem carried the Jewish message of Jesus (whatever that message was thought to have been), and laid it at the feet of Greeks who would modify it with their own speculations. The problem then is not the unreliability of sources, but the absence of all source material. Where are the writings of the original community? Where are the writings of the Hellenist Jews, the Jewish historians, the members of various sects who may have remarked upon the occurrence of this particular community? Nothing exists. Except for the few fragments of texts which have survived from a supposedly Jewish-Ebionite school, and remarks in the Talmud which suggest a very late rabbinic interest in the movement, the first systematic writings we have are those of Gentile Christians, the Church fathers. These formal historical writings completely evict Judaism from the evidence of the Church.

In light of these facts, what Jewish writers interested in Christian beginnings -- and they are numerous -- are left with is an implicit program. I suggest the overriding, if unexpressed, idea which lies behind most, if not all, Jewish studies of Jesus and the early Church is a concern to reduce the elements of Christian faith-statements until there is revealed a "sensible" account of precisely those statements a Jew can have made. I am not referring to a Jewish deduction of that which can be claimed about Jesus. There is no Jewish reclamation of Jesus (see Chapter Eight, below). The focus is rather the reverse: to what extent can one profess divergence and yet remain a Jew. Hence, Jewish studies of Jesus have proliferated since the emancipation. It is not the case, however, that Jews will claim Jesus as "supremely one of their own." To do so risks violation of a cardinal principle of each form of contemporary Judaism: that God alone is to be tendered "outstanding" respect.

If Jews are concerned to delimit Christian faith-statement until they have a content compatible to a non-monolithic, yet core-oriented Judaism, a hermeneutic methodology is implemented. If we do not arrive at what may be deemed the historically accurate presentation of the early followers of Jesus, we may present a coherent image of the proto-Christian (I want to say, "ursprunglich Quelle" -- or "primordial source"). There is, alongside of this concern, a most subtle expression of the idea that Jesus himself cannot have been that which was claimed for him. The Jewish side of this problem, then, is to identify the sourceless source. What is at stake is the very border of Judaism, which is at the same time the frontier of Christianity. (There can be no doubt, however, that Jews should prefer this "frontier Christianity" to the alternative: pagan regression).

In the smaller groups into which we broke to facilitate discussion, the centrality of Jesus was identified immediately as the subject of the text of Acts 4:11-12. The Catholics present asked how contemporary Jews regard the passages about, or the person of, Jesus. The common consensus among the Jews present was that the texts were to be taken literally, that is, understood in their own right, and rejected.

The claim that a passage can be taken literally suggests at least that (1) the words make sense; (2) the phrases are obvious; (3) the meaning is clear; and may further suggest that (4) the passage is indisputable in the whole context of (a) the Bible, (b) one's life, and (c) the universe. These requirements would count as a "positive" literal sense of a text. This positive literalism implies that the passage cannot be improved upon. Yet there is another type of literalism which may be characterized as a "negative" literalism. In this sense, the text may be regarded as basically understandable, but credence is not given the text. Indeed, the subject refuses to think about the text in terms of truth content.

I suggest there is a non-detrimental literalism and a narrow, unthinking literalism, but this overstates my argument. Each person present performed a penultimate interpretation of the passage in question. It is not the case that Acts 4:11-12 is meaningless, senseless, or ignorant. As a feature presentation of the program that evening, the passage had to be made sensible for one to continue to participate in the dialogue. Ultimately, then, I would claim -- in agreement with the priest and the rabbi, in agreement with both Judaism and Catholicism -- that literalism is impossible. A literal attitude may be a necessary first confrontation with a text, but to stay on the literal level is proof that one refuses to think about what one is reading.

Taking a passage literally is a short hand for rejecting the image of Jesus presented, the idea that Jesus was "the only name" through which salvation may be achieved, or, indeed, that any human name can be so regarded. If the claim means what it says, a Jew must reject the claim, and reject the image of Jesus which is a consequence of the claim. Literalism, in fact, contains an immediate interpretation of the passage as something which can be characterized as essentially unrelated to Judaism, and therefore not to be assimilated into a Jewish perspective. The point is that a consistent literalism is impossible. We each must interpret what we confront in terms of our life-circumstances, even so-called literalists.

The implication that the Jews were relatively unwilling to speak their mind, which the leaders of the discussion later said they had expected, was disadvantageous in terms of the implicit requirement for honesty in dialogue.[3] We ought to call an ace "an ace" and a deuce "a deuce." This is not to say that metaphoric content, or even hyperbolic language, ought to be excluded from human discourse. Ambiguity would seem to have a valid place when we are searching for the correct presentation of our thought. This should also be understood by our partner in dialogue. Good conversation must be characterized by continuous statements of the terms of agreement and disagreement until each participant understands the other. This cannot be the case in superficial meetings. Our preconceptions must first be routed. Then our proclivity to immediately interpret the other must be left behind. To be really open to what another is saying seems to demand we confront our confusion and doubt. Hesitancy is an important aspect of discovery. Silence, which may be golden, rarely allows thought to progress, seldom draws out questions which will advance us towards a more definitive statement, or engage us in a conversation which will aid in the freer flow of ideas and insight.

What is objectionable is disingenuous evasion of a true response. What is obnoxious is to be so tactful that one is taken in a manner which does not express one's true opinion. Each of these reactions (or failures to react properly) are closer to "double-talk," or what George Orwell in 1984 called "news peak." He characterized such evasion elsewhere as an attempt "to give an appearance of solidity to pure wind" (Orwell, 162). True conversation is dangerous. One is given over to difference and perplexity, of challenge to that which we may regard as our fundamental beliefs. Nevertheless, the rewards of the risk are great: understanding, cooperation, openness, and commitment to further learning and growth.

One should never be reluctant to state his or her opinion. One should never be afraid to have a minority voice because, the way our world is constructed, at some point everyone finds him- or herself outnumbered. It often turns out to be the case that minority opinion, once refined and properly presented, becomes accepted by the majority. This is not frequently the case, but it is a real possibility. Democratic pluralism and the exercise of rational intelligence overrides both immediate emotionalism and historical obfuscations. One of the great intentions of interfaith dialogues and ecumenical congresses is to emphasize that differences are not detrimental to the confidence we should have in pursuing a satisfactory life.

Jews and Christians have different conceptions of what constitutes the correct relationship with God. Nevertheless, only direct assertion of our claims can become available to more cogent understanding. Further, such honesty should be appreciated as a non-threatening expression of personal perceptions. If so, no offense should be taken. Thus Rahner, who participated in Vatican II, can state: "None of the existing non-Christian religions is an unadulterated expression of the right relationship between God and humanity; each is sinfully deficient also in profound ways." Yet he goes on to remark in parentheses: "It's possible to ask whether something similar isn't true with us" (Rahner, 1968, 135). Our conversations teach that errors in others may also express errors among ourselves.

At the conclusion of the evening, the Priest referred to the freedom with which Catholics speak to Catholics because of an absence of inhibitions. One can speak to one's own in-group without compromising one's values, and with less fear of being misunderstood, and therefore little fear of having the discussion interrupted before one can present one's views, or learn the other's views. Indeed, if the experience of the other participants was anything like that of my wife and myself, the most animate and penetrating discussion occurred in the car ride home. This is an ultimate value of Jewish-Christian conversations. We are given alternative views to think about, points which widen our horizons, factors to confirm our own beliefs, and the ability to grow and understand how another may have beliefs different from our own.

I shall given one example. Several Catholic participants offered their understanding of the Trinity. This served not only to help the Jews understand the admittedly difficult concept, but at the same time to be confirmed in their own Sh'ma.[4] Pluralism is healthy and beneficial. Openness and honesty eventually purge fear and mistrust. We learn more about ourselves and others through conversation, through the give and take of language and thought (not the give or take of rigid cultural convictions).

I cannot help but view some remarks of the priest as a paradigmatic expression of the confusion of the Church. I do not regard the confusion as debilitating, but as a tension between faith and the necessity of accepting the science, technology, and the system of knowledge which anchors daily life in the twentieth century. Dogma, as points of orientation, as definitive of Catholicism, as "fences" against assimilation into the malt of experiences, as focal points of clarification, and so on, are not unique to the Church. Judaism has -- although Jews feel rather freer to debate the fact of their existence as much as their cogency -- cardinal tenets. Our traditional sancta, if you will, conflicts with modern life, no matter how modern a suit we put on in the morning.

The confusion has been presented to me by several acquaintances. Catholics have told me of the chaos which resulted from comparing pre-Vatican II assertions (including, for example, threats of excommunication for not believing the fundamental letter of Church dictates) and the post-Vatican II "liberalized" concern to follow one's conscience within the broad guidelines of the Church's newest interpretations. Catholics, I assume, are no longer told what the Immaculate Conception, for example, means in detail; only that it is a fact. They are offered alternative methods of understanding what the fact may mean. Along these lines, it seems amazing that a Hans Kung or a Henri Lefebvre can criticize one of the most fundamental distinctions of Catholicism, the institution of the Papacy, and escape with relatively lenient reprimands: restrictions, but not excommunication.

Likewise, a Jewish friend has suggested that he does not understand what Catholics think they are doing when searching for their "Jewish roots." He said, although I do not see why this would be the case, that a true understanding of the Jewish rooting of Christianity -- a recognition of the thorough Jewishness of Jesus? -- would require rejection of the Christian Bible, unless it were retained as "an historical relic of one of the ways with which Judaism was introduced to Gentiles." I would not go nearly so far. We cannot legislate for other faiths; we must take them at their word. I would be satisfied with a clearer repudiation of anti-Judaism as a Christian problem (although I have heard as much from our Priest when he stated John was the most "antisemitic" document in the corpus of the Christian Bible, to be ignored as historically obnoxious).[5] I may suggest that the Christian problem with anti-Judaism is not only the inaccurate image of the Jews which is assumed (that Jews, for example, are rejected by God, and as a consequence are lifeless, uncreative, and so on) but anti-Judaism is also an inaccurate assessment of the merciful God which we each worship. Jews would also like to see Vatican recognition of the state of Israel (although I can understand that this may jeopardize Catholic minorities in Arab lands, or even the life of the Pope at the hands of extremists). Finally, Jews would like to see a censure of all Christians who seek to convert Jews. I am willing, for my part, to listen to and act upon Catholic expectations. Given these gestures of seriousness, the two communities can build upon a relationship which recognizes, and may even celebrate, primary differences.

What is recommended is a "minimal" recognition of the integrity of the other community, a respect for their history of communion with, and search for, the trans-human. Yet I think there are maximal expectations as well. It is our responsibility to aid and support the alternative community in world affairs. But there is also a need for open, fair, and honest but critical Jewish interpretations of Christianity. There have been many Christian interpretations of Judaism.[6] Obviously, some are more defective, and others surprisingly insightful. I think Jews owe Christianity the service of offering, but certainly not enforcing, an objective perspective of Christianity. This service would entail criticism of unfair treatment of Jews and others, of obfuscating studies, and of overly tactful (and therefore useless) analyses. The same should be expected from Christian authors.

If I do not myself, as a Jew, define Christianity, there may be the erroneous assumption that anyone who claims to be a Christian is de facto so. If cruel tormentors and anti-redemptionists are permitted to call themselves Christians, then there is no identifiable entity to which the term "Christian" may refer. Christian peoples can rightfully claim that true Christians are those who are informed by love, walk in forgiveness, sanctify their lives in the light of Jesus, and so on.

Insofar as Christians are a proselytizing community, however, their commandment is to bring everyone into the covenant. Hence, sinners -- especially sinners -- are to become Christian. Jesus said: "I did not come to invite virtuous people, but sinners" (Matthew 9:13). Hence, sinners are always invited. I have heard Christian people speak about whether or not the baptism of a particular person "took." This formulation implies an intuitive understanding that at least some of those who, convert or are re-born are not efficaciously Christian. While it is true that Christian people recognize the fact that they are sinners even after the baptism, I refer to a more abstruse error than is confessed by these righteous seekers of forgiveness. The people I have in mind are those who. while claiming to be Christians, do not act in a coherently Christian manner. They may not, for example, see a conflict between holding prejudices and hoping for universal salvation, between spiteful behavior and grace. I do not think it is awkward to call these individuals "pagan," because their praxis is not derived from the Abrahamic covenant. I should be understood: Jews and Muslims also claim to be in covenanted relationship which stems from Abraham. If the behavior of Jews and Muslims is not such as would reflect the approval of God for Abraham, they too should be censured.

Paul bade Christians to "fill your thoughts" with "all that is true, all that is noble, all that is just and pure, all that is lovable and gracious, whatever is excellent and admirable" (Philippians 4:8). These character traits seems adequately to characterize Abraham as he is portrayed in Jewish, Christian and Muslim literature. A Christian, as one who participates in the Abrahamic covenant, is one with thoughts and subsequent deeds as full as these virtues. The self-definition (proof-by-action) of a Christian is a virtuous being. This does not, of course, mean that a Christian, or any human, is exempt from error. Yet Abraham stands as our messenger who bode the distinction between pagan error and his children who, as the Bible adequately shows, may sin, but have the means for overcoming their sins.

God loves the sinner not because of the sin, but because of what God can do with the sinner. If so, the process of recreating the sinner is an ongoing process. God, in other words, is never finished with any particular individual or group once and for all. What we in religious terms call "getting religion" may in secular terms be called "maturity" or "development."

The Jew is needed to identify and criticize the pagan in the midst of the Christian people. The Jew has performed this function since the first days of the Church. Although the Rabbis of that era were hostile critics of the Church, there should be no doubt that the service I am recommending is to be performed out of respect. Jews should regard the connotations presented in the term "Christian" seriously, and be willing to defend what the term designates. Jews ought to be willing and able to defend the people who describe themselves as Christian. This essence of Christianity, as suggested, is that which Christian people themselves present as their own best image: a being of love, accepting and dispensing forgiveness, and so on.

If such were to become the case, Jews would also criticize Jews, and Christians would debate with Christians in a new kind of dialectic, a renewed impartiality, in defence of the other community (if only, as it were, in interpretation). To a certain extent, such cross-cultural, disinterested studies occur in our day. I am thinking of Franz

Rosenzweig, Martin Buber, and others in the Jewish community.[7] I recommend the practice become conscious and extended. Entailed in such a practice would be the freedom to be oneself coupled with a freedom to study the other objectively. Each community would, then, benefit. We would, as it were, be more at ease in the car ride home.

NOTES

1. Inasmuch as the term "antisemitism" was used by the Priest, I allow it to stand in his comments. In fact, "antisemitism" is a recent (19th century) term which designates social or political hostility against Jews. The appropriate term when discussing early Christian assertions about the Jews would have been "anti-Judaism" or "anti-Jewishness." The first is commonly accepted as a term referring to assertions against the religion or culture of the Jewish people. This verbal distinction does raise the issue of the relations between the earliest followers of Jesus -- all of whom were Jews -- and the composition of the Church at the extreme point of rupture with organized Judaism. I believe that the Priest may have chosen to use the term "antisemitism," -- though his seminary training should have told him that the term referred to socio-political hostility, and would have been an anachronism in our present context -- because both Judaism and Catholicism seem to share a commitment to the idea that the cultural/religious realm cannot be radically separated from the social/political. If so, the practical treatment of Jews which derived from the theological writing of the Church fathers does constitute social/political hostility (an issue treated in a superior manner by Father Flannery). The Patristic writings, however, were not investigated at the dialogue session and are only relevant insofar as they were inspired directly from the writings of the early Church.

2. Acts 2:46-47a: "With one mind they kept up their daily attendance at the temple, and, breaking bread in private houses, shared their meals with unaffected joy, as they praised God and enjoyed the favor of the whole people." This passage clearly says the earliest followers of Jesus were Jewish, temple-worshippers who were respected by the whole people of Israel (including, no doubt, the Pharisees who defended them from the Sadducees!). I see no reason why Luke, historian of the separation, would have invented such compatibility.

3. For an excellent statement of what dialogue is (and is not) see Kelley and Olson (esp. pp. 7ff) and the works recommended in their bibliography.

4. The Sh'ma, from Deuteronomy 6:4ff, is considered the fundamental creed of Judaism (from which all other regulations and commandments follow). The essential service states: "Hear, O Israel, the Lord our God, the Lord, is One." An alternative interpretation is: "Hear, Israel, the Lord God is One."

5. After this paper was published, I was privileged to see "The Word in Anguish: Wrestling with Anti-Judaism in the Lectionary," a video made by, and available from, the Cincinnati Archdiocese. "The Word in Anguish" deals with the issue of antisemitism/anti-Judaism as a problem for the Church.

6. For Christian interpretations of Judaism see Flannery, Fox, Herford, Moehlman, and especially the extensive meditations of Van Buren. The introductory chapter of Van Buren (1987) consists in part of a discussion of authors whose works were a preliminary discussion of the Church's recognition of Jews and Judaism. His criticisms of these authors seems beneficial to advancing Church-Synagogue relations, but he does not give enough credit to these theologians who were forging their thoughts virtually without the benefit of a precedent. It seems to me that Christian theologians and scholars cannot be expected to make a radical leap from our historical relations to a detailed elaboration of our mutual relations of the future. Nor should Christian authors be expected to vacillate on statements concerning their own heritage. Inasmuch as dialogue requires respect for the other as well as self-respect, these early authors should be appreciated as courageous as well as insightful. I maintain that our dialogue is at the beginning, and that there is much work to be done on both sides and for both sides. Nevertheless, what has begun since the early 1960's is amazing and awe-inspiring when one considers what had gone before we began discussions, with each other in sincerity and with honesty. The earliest theologians of dialogue -- both Jewish and Christian -- have been forging what amounts to a new ethic (a renewal of taking seriously their own foundational ethics).

7. For Jewish statements of an interpretative nature about Christianity, see Baeck, Buber, Fackenheim, Rubenstein, and especially the penetrating insights of Rosenzweig (and the listing in the work cited under Rosenstock-Huessy and Rosenzweig). Rosenzweig, more than any Jewish author before him and most after, attempted to take seriously the self-definitive statements of both Judaism and Christianity. The result of his labors was the development of an unparalleled monument to the relatedness in diversity between the two religions. Rosenzweig is worth reading carefully, even though his thought is often dense and complex. It will take quite a bit of work to advance beyond his contributions to the reality of the Jewish and Christian conversation. His biography is also quite interesting. For this, see Glatzer.

Chapter Seven

Two Popular Jewish Interpretations of Jesus

In this chapter I investigate two recent interpretations of Jesus of Nazareth. Each of the texts investigated, Pinchas Lapide's The Resurrection of Jesus and Ellis Rivkin's What Crucified Jesus, are ultimately concerned with issues of Jewish Christian relations. If my arguments are cogent, I show that neither Lapide nor Rivkin can be taken as role models in Jewish-Christian dialogue. Each author attributes adulated imagery to the person of Jesus, yet neither satisfactorily responds to the Christian image of Jesus.

Pinchas Lapide on the Resurrection of Jesus

Lapide, an Israeli citizen, has written several easy to read and, as a result, popular works. Although several years old, The Resurrection of Jesus is readily accessible, and promotes a particular understanding which may be appealing to the popular imagination. If, then, we find in Lapide's work an example of a general problem in this genre of literature, our criticism will be valuable. In general, our authors' works are interesting and well-reasoned. In this particular example, I claim Lapide obfuscates the issue.

Lapide says he can "accept neither the messiahship of Jesus for the people of Israel nor the Pauline interpretation of the resurrection of Jesus" (153). If, as he claims throughout his text, he is concerned with dialogue, I question what kind of dialogue can be based on obfuscation.

Christianity holds that Jesus was, and is, the Messiah, and rose on the third day after his death. According to Christians, these dictum are inseparable. Yet Lapide desires to emphasize one of the doctrines, the resurrection, and ignore the other, the Messiahship. He presumes this will contribute to Jewish-Christian dialogue.

Lapide tells us that the event of the resurrection is nowhere described as a miracle, nor "as an event of salvation, or as a deed of God, a fact which tends to support the plausibility of the report for the disinterested reader" (100). Yet this statement raises more questions than it offers solutions.

If the resurrection is not explicitly called a "miracle," what else can it be called? If, indeed, it was not a miracle, does this not give authority to the doctrine that the event was a natural act, perhaps planned before the creation of the world? It also seems to be the case that the prophecies prior to the event do categorize the resurrection as a miracle, and a salvation event. Further, the very report of a resurrection deters any disinterest. The propaganda value of reporting the resurrection, or the value-free assertion of the event either assumes it was a miracle, or that it figures in the scheme of salvation. Otherwise, we may question the purpose of the resurrection. Certainly Paul viewed the resurrection of Jesus in salvational terms. Christ, he says repeatedly, "died for our sins."

Indeed, Lapide himself supports the contention that the death and resurrection of Jesus was inherently salvational, as sponsoring faith in God. He says the resurrection of Jesus "became for his disciples on that day of ruin a theological imperative which was demanded by their never completely forgotten confidence in God" (89). The death of Jesus, then, was a test of the disciples faith in God.

Yet on another lever, the perspective of the resurrection of Jesus was salvational in a larger sense, in the sense that it demanded the disciples argue -- with God -- for justice. Belief in Jesus' value as a messianic figure, and disbelief in his death, required that the disciples act according to a well-established Jewish motif which ran from Abraham through the Hasidim of modern European background. Lapide says it was "just as legitimate for Peter and his friends to dispute with [H]im [God] as it was for the patriarch of Israel." As we remember, Abraham argued against God, "Shall not the judge of all the earth do right?" (Gen. 18:25). Lapide relates these two demands with the insight that each found a response in Heaven.

This is an interesting argument, but is not supported in the Christian documents. According to these records, the disciples were surprised and shocked by the death of Jesus, but the report of his resurrection brought equal astonishment and skepticism. Eventually the disciples came to believe that Jesus was indeed raised from the dead. They came to believe, in other words, that "the resurrection belongs to the category of the truly real and effective occurrences, for without a fact of history there is no true act of faith." Lapide makes the above assertion even though he is willing to grant that, "in accordance with the spirit of that epoch," the report of the resurrection was surrounded by "a dense wreath of legends" (92-3).

Since Lapide calls the resurrection a "fact of history," one must question what he means when he says that the "resurrection of Jesus was ambiguous as an event." It is clear what he means when he says that the resurrection was "unambiguous in the history of its effect" (144). This means, quite simply, that people will act on a premise whether or not that premise is true, and that the consequences of their actions are real whether or not the ideology behind their actions is correct.

Lapide concludes that the resurrection was, in the last analysis, "an experience of God which enters into the realm of things which cannot be proved" (31). This statement is acceptable. It may be the case that nothing asserted about God or actions in history can or should be proved. They are either to be believed and acted upon, or not believed and, and some would say, the consequences of disbelief accepted. Yet Lapide would go on to restrict any form of decision on this matter. He comes out against the argument which would attempt to "understand 'reality' in a restricted way, exclusively as a physically comprehensible or rationally understandable facticity - a standard which is hostile to all human faith" (43).

Several comments deserve mention. In the first place, the criteria of empirical investigation and rational assessment are primarily standards which are hostile to all illusion, madness and ineptitude. We should not suggest that faith is one of these. Faith may be more efficacious and necessary than reason in certain instances. One may think, for example, of a man marooned on an island in the middle of the ocean. Faith may help him survive until assistance arrives. By the same token, reason will aid him in gathering food and supplies which are immediate needs to be fulfilled before one can, or should, worry about if or when salvation will arrive.

In the second place, our entire culture and way of life is premised upon, supported by, and advanced with scientific practice. When we think of any boon to civilization -- for example, better agricultural techniques which feed millions of people, computer games which may be designed to teach polity and moral values, entertainments and comforts -- few people recommend we do away with empirical investigation and rational analysis or their results. We may complain because monies are not efficaciously applied to problems. That is a different issue.

Third, the scientific attitude and method have no direct bearing on God or religion. Commitment to God ought to include open-eyed assessment of the world in which we live. We ought to understand both what needs to be done and what cannot be accomplished. Faith must include the premise (or promise) that if we act on good intentions and to the best of our ability to do that which is right, God will not pour out wrath upon us. If we act as if technological and scientific advancements are either unimportant or positively damaging, we destroy an important distinction. If we bemoan the condition of the world instead of recognizing that which can be changed for the better, and that which can be utilized to improve values and sensibilities, we will find ourselves in a position where we cannot tell mere physical and technological phenomena from that which is truly important. If we negate the distinction between scientific method and scientific madness we are well along the road of confusing God-seeking with insanity. We should not draw distinctions so tightly.

Lapide says: "I cannot believe in the empty tomb nor in the angels in white garments," nor other embellishments which were the creation of later generations who "tried to whip up enthusiasm" (128). In what sense is the empty tomb an embellishment? How can assertion of an empty tomb whip up support? It seems, rather, the empty tomb is the most basic fact which can be asserted with regard to the resurrection of Jesus. The empty tomb in itself means very little. What is significant is the importance attached to it in confessional terms. The report of the empty tomb is the most believable statement. The documents themselves, however, indicate that this mere fact can be used either for the Christian message or against it. The empty tomb may mean either that Jesus was resurrected, or that the disciples, or someone else, stole the body.

The rabbis tell a story about a resurrection which happened to one of their own. Two friends, both sages and righteous men, became too drunk at a celebration, and one rabbi inadvertently killed his partner. God, however, raised the dead man on petition from the distraught murderer. Lapide quotes this story as evidence that bodily resurrection is not inconceivable (50, 131). However, Lapide ignores the corrective aspect of the Talmud's report. The tale goes on to tell how, the following year, the first rabbi invited his friend to again celebrate. The latter declined, saying: "perhaps a miracle may not occur twice." If this story indicates that bodily resurrection is possible, then it also indicates that bodily resurrection was considered to be a miracle. The point is that miracles are not to be relied upon nor anticipated. Miracles, then, function as a teaching tool. In this story we have a miracle report which instructs us not to rely on miracles! The issue may depend on what the resurrection of Jesus was meant to teach. This is a question Lapide does not satisfactorily address. Perhaps it is one to which a Jew cannot respond.

As an orthodox Jew, Lapide may say the resurrection was a fact, but must conclude that this "fact" means nothing to Jews. It is the case, however, that all facts mean something! If the resurrection of Jesus means something to Lapide, he ought to tell us what that might be. Yet if the resurrection of Jesus does have meaning to Lapide it is difficult to imagine how he can consider himself an orthodox Jew. According to orthodox Jews, Torah means something, and Torah means everything. Yet if the resurrection of Jesus, whether a "fact" of some kind or not, means nothing, why write a book on the subject?

Lapide asserts that, as a faithful Jew, he cannot explain the historical development which, "despite many errors and much confusion, has carried the central message of Israel from Jerusalem into the world of the nations" (142). Yet he wants to avoid saying the beginning of the missionizing Church was either conscious contrivance or mass delusion. These suggestions may be avoided if we make the following assumptions. Like all righteous people, Jesus was expected to rise at the End of Days. The idea that Jesus will rise is acceptable to both Jew and Christian. The issue of Jesus' already having risen is the problematic point. The earliest first-hand report we have of a person having seen Jesus is contained in the vision of Paul. If we admit the notion that a vision may run the gamut from illusion to keen insight, intellectual discernment or intuition, all contention is put aside until this question is resolved. If Paul had a vision of the risen Jesus, this vision carries as much or as little weight as Paul himself attributed to it. There is, and can be, no proof of a vision. Indeed, if Paul had a vision, or if any other disciple had a vision, they may legitimately spread their message of the vision and the significance of the vision. The issue of the reality of the resurrection is not broached. Paul and others, of course, would say the vision reports a real historical event.

This is not inherent in the facts at hand. Indeed, the utility of a vision is to be severely qualified. It is no more or less efficacious than acting on a vision of a talking unicorn.

This is not to say that the vision of Jesus, or the faith in Jesus as practiced by Christian peoples today is vacuous. Rather, Christians -- as well as Jews, Moslems, atheists, and others -- are judged on their actions, not their beliefs. Beliefs cannot be proven. And, as suggested above, they are not meant to be subjected to empirical analysis or rational assessment.

Our author himself places Jesus' resurrection in non-specified ideological terms, that is, terms supposed to be acceptable to both Jews and Christians. Lapide interprets 1 Peter 3:18 as follows: Jesus "also died...a righteous one [among] others." Thus the verse indicates, according to Lapide, that the disciples expected from Jesus what Jews had always expected of their martyrs -- vicarious representation (145). This idea in itself does not inherently demand we believe in either the bodily resurrection of the martyr nor the messiahship of the man. Furthermore, insofar as this representation suggests some form of vicarious action -- whether it be vicarious atonement, vicarious argument in the upper worlds, or whatnot -- analysis is required. Certainly the earliest disciples of Jesus did not imagine a christological self-repentance of God. Rather, if Lapide is right in his correlation of the disciples with Abraham, the disciples perceived themselves in an adversarial situation wherein the righteous plead and harrow God on behalf of the children of Israel.

It is not difficult to argue, from this suggestion, the ease with which the Jewish understanding of Jesus' friends passed through permutations which made the original message understandable to the nations. Without a doubt, this brought the pagan closer to God. Yet a Jew who calls himself orthodox, or any Jew who holds the revelations to Israel true in some sense, may see here a call to develop a Jewish theology of "Christology" which would, as it were, purge the recognition of Jesus of all his unnatural, un-Jewish attributes. This Jewish analysis of Christian premises and beliefs may even require a limitation of the sense of Jesus' resurrection. I have suggested that Jesus' adventure after death was not delusion, but the case of loving friends demanding of God that the beloved teacher not be eternally dismissed. This suggestion was taken from Lapide's otherwise confused involvement with peripheral issues.

Lapide thinks "the Church stands and falls with the resurrection of Jesus" (144). It may be the case that the Church herself thinks she stands or falls on this single issue, but the statement is too facile. The reality of the Church is more complicated than such simplification allows. The Church stands or falls as a community of persons seeking both God and righteousness. In this they differ neither from individual Jews nor any person concerned with what may be termed human welfare in all its aspects. In these terms, the bodily resurrection of Jesus is negligible. As a teaching tool, however, the resurrection may guide believers in any number of directions.

Lapide asks, "would it not be unbiblical arrogance to suggest to unnumbered millions of God-believing Christians that their faith rests on a falsification, an error, a figment of the imagination?" (144). It would! Yet this is suggested most subtly when Lapide himself claims that the resurrection was a "fact," but the "fact" of the resurrection is not the "fact" which millions of Christians in various churches believe. As suggested above, a Jew may forthrightly deny that Jesus was resurrected, yet allow that the story has heuristic value for Christians. Of course, Christians believe Jesus was resurrected in fact, that he was the Messiah, and that these two assertions cannot be distinguished. Jesus' Messiahship is embodied in his resurrection and vice-versa. The greater arrogance is to pretend to agree with a position, yet deny it. The greater arrogance is to think something erroneous, yet not speak about the error in a text devoted to the issue. Honesty is the best ecumenical policy. In the long run, both sides will benefit.

It seems to be true that the attitude which makes one a Christian or a Jew, an atheist, a Buddhist, or a scientist and a lawyer, is "faith," understood to mean both an active confidence and a confident acting. Faith, in these terms, means striving after righteousness, to the best of one's ability, with the best of intentions, through rational inquiry, pursuit of the most trenchant forms of justice, holding dear the idea of our humility, with courage, and so on. In this regard, neither the idea of Jesus' resurrection, nor the detailed specification of the requirements of Torah are essential.

Relational insight refers to our living together, not believing separately. Jewish-Christian relations contain the idea of doing justice to each group of peoples, and every individual, who is seeking understanding. Lapide's work is a step in the direction of true ecumenical confidence. In light of this, the minor criticisms I have raised are unimportant. One day we will reach the paradoxical stage when not only everything we say will be fundamentally correct, but at the same time will not be indicative of contention. On that day, scholarly papers will be both unafflicted by special interests, yet still interesting and important. Such a day may seem to be a utopian dream in view of contemporary newspaper headlines. Yet for all that, we ought not cease striving for genuine relationships, even if some strive for it under different names. Call it "the End of Days," the "Day of the Lord," the "Kingdom of Heaven," "Utopia," or whatever. What seems important is that we contribute in that direction.

Lapide has done so.

Ellis Rivkin on the Charismatic of Charismatics

Ellis Rivkin's book, What Crucified Jesus, is to be appreciated for its clear and concise presentation of the political conditions which prevailed in the time of Jesus. His question concerning "what" crucified Jesus can be criticized as fudging the issue of responsibility in Jesus' death. The question of responsibility is not required for placing blame or assigning guilt, but for understanding an historical incident. Rivkin, perhaps in spite of his formation of the question, has provided us with an analysis enabling us to locate responsibility where it certainly existed: with Pilate.

Jesus must have assessed the conditions through which his teaching occurred as fraught with danger. There is a continual tension in the texts between what a "right thinking," that is apathetic, person might do, and what Jesus was proposing. Jesus preached a message of the kingdom to come, a kingdom claimed to be superior to the present earthly kingdom (i.e. Rome). Jesus at least tacitly recommended the replacement of Roman oppression. Jesus empowered his followers to be the bearers and bringers of the Kingdom of God. The very act of preaching such a message placed Jesus at odds with the power of Rome. The empowerment of his followers constituted an act of rebellion.

Rivkin begins his discussion by noting that the Jewish historian Josephus, while having no love of Zealots, charismatics and others who disturbed the fragile peace, does mention John the Baptist in a respectful manner. Jesus himself is referred to only as the brother of James the Just, and as one who is called "the Christ." The absence of an extended discussion of Jesus is curious. We may grant for the sake of argument that Jesus was remembered by the historian, but the memory is not an appropriate bit of historical information. It tells us nothing. Or, indeed, it suggests that John the Baptist and James the Just were more memorable and deserved mention before Jesus. This surprising fact has led a majority of commentators to deny that Josephus himself penned the comments about "the Christ." Yet the opposite point might also be made. If Jesus is treated as secondary to the Baptist or James, it may be the case that one of *their* followers inserted the phrase, and not a Christian.

Rivkin finds that Josephus' silence about Jesus "stimulates us to try our hand at painting a portrait of the missing charismatic of charismatics from the pigments of the age which Josephus has preserved in his palette" (71). The painting of a superlative charismatic is the weakest point in Rivkin's text. It amounts to an assumption that the Jesus of history, the Jesus in the synoptic accounts, was a charismatic; indeed, the greatest in all of history.

Chapter Five of What Crucified Jesus speaks of a hypothetical charismatic character, and the political machinations which would have evolved if he had performed as Jesus is reported to have acted. This method accounts Jesus as a charismatic before the point is properly argued. Indeed, from the silence of Josephus, the assumption cannot be made. Josephus, or an interpolator, reported two facts about Jesus, each of which could be derived from other, more complete, sources: that Jesus was the brother of James the Just, and that some people called him "the Christ." Neither of these facts lend themselves to the categorical assertion that Jesus was a charismatic.

A separate, but related tactic, is to portray "a charismatic of charismatics out of the matrix of time, structure, process and causality" (94) which was the Judaism of that transitional period. Rivkin's facsimile of Jesus is drawn, rather, from pure speculation. A picture could as easily have been drawn of a Zealot Jesus (or a para-Zealot, as in the works of S.G.F. Brandon), an apocalyptically minded seer, a disciple of Hillel (or, alternatively, Shammai), a Samarian, an Essene, a Hellenist, and so on. Texts have been published which argue that Jesus was a Hindu! The evidence exists as little, or as much, for one as any other. What would be unique, and perhaps closer to the truth, would be an argument that Jesus was an original religious thinker. My assertion does neither praise nor condemn him on that account.

A more realistic method would have been for Rivkin to argue that the Jesus of the synoptics, whose "portraits are so at variance" (91) was a charismatic figure. Considering the "variance," however, this would seem difficult to accomplish. Rivkin seems to unnecessarily congest the issue, if not undermine his own assumptions, when he states, "we do not draw upon those features that are not identical [between the synoptics and his own assumptions], though we make no claim that there are not other features as well" (110). The analysis of any historical character must call upon the accumulated evidence of all the moods, turns, and utterances reported of that character. It will then be the task of the historian to accept appropriate data on a reasoned basis. Rivkin does not do this. As a result, his presentation is marred.

Two flaws adhere to Rivkin's assumption of Jesus as the charismatic of charismatics. In the first place, the figure under discussion is presented without an historical matrix, without legitimate contemporaries. In the second place, Rivkin offers no definition of the type of personality under discussion. He does relate the peoples' perception of Jesus to a prophet-like figure (94), but this Biblical image does not fully encompass the impressions and sensibilities of the latter age in which Jesus lived. Rivkin does not, in other words, cite contemporary examples of charismatic figures in Judaism, as does Geza Vermes in Jesus the Jew; nor does Rivkin provide an analysis of the type of charismatic figure Jesus may have been, as Martin Hengel argues in The Charismatic Leader and His Followers.

Related only to Biblical prototypes -- Moses, Elijah, "one of the prophets" -- Jesus is suggested to be virtually without peer. The exception may be John the Baptist. Yet the portrayal of John differs drastically between the synoptics and Josephus. The former presents the death of the Baptist in terms of religious necessity; the latter in political terms.

There is as little evidence for the unargued assumption that John was a charismatic as there is for assuming that Jesus was a charismatic. Yet even the possibility of a contemporary charismatic companion is questioned by Rivkin. He says, "John may indeed have been a charismatic like Jesus, but he had kept his charisma within acceptable bounds" (99). Hence, the most likely candidate for a peer for Jesus is placed in doubt. This is unfortunate if only because it bypasses the more interesting and more relevant question of how the historical Jesus differed from, for example, Honi the Circle-Drawer, Rabbi Hanina ben Dosa and Pinhas ben Yair. These last three had "contained" their "charisma" so diligently that they are remembered and accepted participants in the Rabbinic enterprise, as John was not. We should also wonder what a contained charisma means.

The discussion of Vermes is much more satisfying in this regard, and should perhaps be read as a necessary complement to Rivkin's text. With Vermes, there is a genuine link between Jesus and other men of his generation. Vermes presents a series of charismatic figures who constituted, in his words, "a northern phenomenon" which was likely to have had "Galilean roots." Vermes adds that the "unsophisticated religious ambiance of Galilee was apt to produce holy men of the Hasidic type" (Vermes 79-80).

Rivkin does use the writings of Josephus or Luke to suggest that Theudas (cf., Acts 5:36) and the Egyptian "prophet" (Acts 21:38) were charismatic figures. Here again the question of type is missing. How might the question of delusions of grandeur apply to such diverse figures as Jesus and Isaiah, Hanina ben Dosa or Theudas? Why is John the Baptist not remembered by Judaism while the equally fiery, equally splendid Simon ben Yohai is accounted among her finest sons? It is disquieting that Rivkin lumps together detested "false prophets" with both the masters of Judaism and the mentors of Christianity. There are clearly differences between the "charisma" of Theudas, of Jesus, and of Honi. But these issues are not discussed.

The leveling of diverse figures, and various times and place, under a single head is not particularly cogent. Rivkin says the charismatics were against violence (which need not necessarily be true of all charismatics -- assuming that Napoleon was someone with "charisma"), built no revolutionary organizations (think of Marx or Freud or, indeed, Jesus), but rather "urged the people to repent and to wait for the coming of God's kingdom" (59). In Rabbinic literature we do not hear of Honi, for example, bidding his contemporaries to wait patiently for the coming of the kingdom.

Without a discussion of types of charismatic figures, we cannot know how precisely to characterize Jesus, or whether he possessed such a personality. Was Jesus essentially a visionary, or one who engaged in dialectical subtleties, one who screamed and shouted praise and condemnation alternatively, or one whose anger at sinful mankind scorched the earth out of the cave? Can a character with "charisma" not possess eyes which light with humor and whose voice softly intones the joy of salvation he or she perceives? Given the contrasts of personalities with various types and degrees of appeal and diligence, what can a "charismatic of charismatics" mean? The question which should be asked is what made Jesus different.

Rivkin is not in a position to answer this question. Given the terms of his presentation, he cannot distinguish between memories of disciples who carried their master into the Gentile world and, for contrast, a figure like Honi, whose disciples carried their memory within Judaism. Rivkin cannot distinguish between the profile of a Jesus who figures in prophecies, and a figure like Abba Hilkiah, who spoke as one of the elders of Judaism. Finally, Rivkin's presentation of Jesus as the "charismatic of charismatics" compels us to view Jesus as a "personality of personalities." If so, it is difficult to assess the personality of Jesus without comparison to someone like Simon ben Yohai who, while always distinct, has always been viewed as a teacher in Israel. The question can only be raised here, not answered. The reason for this failure to characterize Jesus is undoubtedly the lack of information about him.

Perhaps Rivkin bypasses the more interesting question of distinguishing traits of Jesus because he smooths over the sharp edges in the puzzle of Judaism, Christianity, and their relations. Rivkin flirts with Christian phraseology. This is suggested by his invention of the term "charismatic of charismatics." The rhetoric suggests superiority. However, superiority cannot be established, for Jesus or anyone else, without discussing difference and similarities.

Conclusion

There is certainly nothing wrong with Jewish authors who investigate Christian history, ideology or culture. I suggested above that more is required of Jewish authors. Yet even the minimal analyses are best accomplished when the differences between the two are honestly faced. If an author finds something praiseworthy in another culture, he or she ought to explicate it. However, calling Jesus a charismatic, and proceeding to suggest that he was the greatest ever to live, benefits neither Judaism nor Christianity.

If the category of "charisma" is not vacuous, it is certainly a category of "personality" for which Judaism both has candidates and eschews as a relevant category. The question which may be most relevant to an historian is why the Jewish charismatics remained Jewish, and why the "charisma" of Jesus was carried to the nations.

It is on these terms, perhaps, that Jews and Christians can discuss personalities.

If a common theme is shared by Lapide and Rivkin, it is the assumption of an appreciative term, the giving of a favorable impression, for the person of Jesus. The Charismatic of Charismatics (Rivkin) or the (implicit notion of a) Resurrected One (Lapide) are viewed by Christians as superlative terms when applied to Jesus. Such imagery implies adoration, or at least uniqueness which cannot be claimed (because of want of information, or competing figures who are not discussed). Inasmuch as our authors will not allow adoration or uniqueness to any human being, both Lapide and Rivkin must ultimately reject their own designations of Jesus.

Chapter Eight

Is There a Jewish Reclamation of Jesus?

Jesus as a Theme for Jewish Thinkers

The most cursory reading of Jewish authors on the person and History of Jesus ought to indicate that there is no single "Jewish point of view" on these themes. If this is true, there cannot be a singular creedal position on the Jewish relation to the memory of Jesus, nor a unified program of assessment. Each of these points is implicitly denied in the title of Donald Hagner's The Jewish Reclamation of Jesus.

In this paper, I argue that there is no uniform perspective which deserves the name "reclamation." My contention is that Hagner has chosen an inappropriate word as the title of a text which otherwise conveys several cogent criticisms of various Jewish analyses of Jesus. We begin with an issue which seems to contain the very antithesis of Jewish and Christian statements concerning Jesus.

Hagner asserts, "What must be said as forcefully as possible is that the kerygmatic Christ of the Gospels is fully Jewish. Acceptance of the entire narrative of the Gospel tradition entails no denial of Jesus' Jewishness" (84). He clearly desires to dissolve the distinction between the kerygmatic Christ and the historical Jesus. Jewish authors, by contrast, unanimously agree that the distinction must stand. In this manner, they may comfortably speak about the historical Jesus without being compelled to make pronouncements on the Christ figure. Hagner's statement is composed of two premises: (a) that the kerygmatic Christ is Jewish, and (b) that one need not deny Jesus' Jewishness if the "entire narrative of the Gospel tradition" is accepted. It is noteworthy that the positive form of point (b) cannot be maintained, to wit, that acceptance of the Gospel tradition entails acceptance of Jesus' Jewishness. Jesus' Jewishness seems obvious to us today, but even at the turn of the century the statement was controversial. Hence, if point (b) is true, it is trivial.

As to point (a), this may mean either of two things: (i) that the kerygmatic Christ of the gospels is a Jewish being, or (ii) that the kerygmatic Christ is a Jewish idea. Hagner indicates that the second is the correct interpretation of his thought. He says the kerygmatic Christ idea is "not intrinsically alien to the faith of Israel" (84). I assume that Hagner does not recommend with this comment that Jews can remain Jews and accept the kerygmatic Christ. If Jews will not give consideration to the kerygmatic being, this leaves us with an historical question. The fact that, historically, Jews did not accept the Christ indicates that not being intrinsically alien is not determinative. The very least that is suggested is that most Jews saw no acceptable positive criteria which was to guide their decision toward acceptance of Jesus as the Christ. Further, the idea of Jesus as the Christ seems limited to the Hellenistic, or even more exclusively, the Philonic school of Jews. The fact that the proclaimed Jesus was not the accepted Jesus cuts a distinction between the announcement of the dawning of the kingdom and the empirically based denial of the claim.

Elsewhere Hagner refers to the Jewish "zeal to keep Jesus within Judaism, either as one who presented the culmination of its religious teaching or simply as a misled Israelite" (67). I submit, first of all, that the use of the word "keep" negates any need for "reclamation." Further, I deny that any Jewish author has referred to Jesus as the culmination of Jewish teachings. This is not only a Christian claim but, as we shall see below, the implicit Jewish denial of such a claim is a matter of contention for Hagner. Finally, I wonder whether Jews who expend as much energy and ink on Jesus (as have Jewish scholars in our time) in order to retain or reclaim a "misled Israelite" would not themselves be misguided. To the best of my knowledge, no modern Jewish author has claimed that Jesus was misguided. The extremes are equally as great, however, in that Jesus has been suggested to be insignificant as well as a genius.

Hagner does not quote one of his seven primary subjects, nor any of his dozen or so secondary subjects, with the exception of Joseph Klausner, as forthrightly claiming reclamation of Jesus. And there is good reason for failing to have done so. The Jewish authors have, almost exclusively, limited themselves to historical questions. By concentrating on the Jesus of history, Jews categorically reject the claims of Christology. Claims rejected can in no sense be deemed a form of reclamation. In fact, Hagner quotes Sandmel as explicitly repudiating the unfortunate suggestion of "Klausner's distant dream of a reclaimed Jesus" (quoted, 262). If there is a single point which finds agreement among all Jews, it is expressed in Hagner's assessment of the Jewish conviction "that the kingdom has not come in any real sense, and this forces Jews to reject the teachings of Christianity about Jesus" (135). I submit that rejection and reclamation are mutually exclusive.

Jewish Analyses of Jesus

Hagner's complaint that the Jewish picture of Jesus "does not do justice to the portrait of him contained in the Gospels" (269) seems misdirected. The Jewish claim is that the portrait contained in the documents in question do not do justice to the Galilean Jew who lived and died under the oppressive Roman occupation of Israel. The demand to accept a text as it stands, while not necessarily intellectually dishonest, is asserted only on issues where there is possible division. It is a partisan demand. There is no question concerning whether or not to accept the text of Macbeth as it stands. Nor could we expect any Jew to agree to accept the forgeries called The Protocols of the Elders of Zion as they stand. But we are not dealing with singularly sublime production such as Macbeth, nor with an obviously depraved work like the Protocols. We are dealing with a work which grew out of not one, but several oral traditions, which had been coalesced at least four times, and which had been redacted and editorialized any number of times. If one prefers a paradox: in the text we have, we do not possess the text as it stands. We have several valorous visions and statements of hope. But none of these are coherent in terms of the Jewish vision, nor in Jewish statements of hope.

The statement that the Jesus documents contain "the only historical sources about Jesus that we possess" (269) needs argument. In fact, the Church fathers have handed down fragments from the Ebionites, who may have been closer to Jesus than were Stephen or Paul. What became of their works is perhaps a political question. Further, it may be the case that study is required into the historical kernels which can be gathered from the Rabbinic literature (although the collected works of Herford, and Morris Goldstein's Jesus in the Jewish Tradition, and others, have gone far in this regard). Finally, consideration ought be given the absence of any legitimate references in the works of Josephus, and the disappearance of documents from the fellowship in Jerusalem which would seem to have been valuable and worthy of preservation.

In fact, Hagner would allow no critical assessment of the texts. He writes as if Jewish analyses are based entirely on subjective criterion, that Jews pick and choose randomly that which will bolster their case. I submit there is a more coherent and principled method behind the authors who write about the historical Jesus. An objective study would be able to unearth the critical criteria and assess them in their own terms. This will not be done in the present essay. I will only mention that there is no fundamental contradiction between a document and determination that something other lies behind the document. It is as if, for example, I visit Corinth and see the stark remains of the Temple of Apollo. I can claim that the structure is unreliable as a housing but can, by a process of "mental excavation," understand what was once there.

The "Liberal" Concern With Jesus

Hagner is essentially correct when he says "the impetus for the modern Jewish study of Jesus comes almost exclusively from the Liberal wing of Judaism," and the reason given is that for these Jews "only ethical teachings are relevant to the modern age" (142). It is noteworthy that ethical utterances in Judaism are not halachic but haggadic. They are, to be too brief, not authoritative, but applicable to the variety and flux of situations. Judaism indeed holds that there is an eternal set of values which are immutable. Any verbalization of this everlasting norm, however, is attached to language, and shares the ambiguity and versatility of that human form.

I suspect that the Liberal concern with Jesus has a specific intention. Considering that the Reform movement in general began in the early nineteenth century, the works of Klausner and Montefiore in the early to mid twentieth century cannot be said to be a dramatic leap. Further, the real explosion of Jewish interest in Jesus is under twenty years old. The names of Vermes, Flusser, Sandmel, and perhaps Lapide represent a literal doubling of the earlier important authors (Lapide, it should be noted, is an Orthodox Jew). Along with the interest in Jesus comes a critical stance towards Jewish ritual. As Judaism became no longer a national assembly, but a religious fellowship, ethics was proposed as the spiritual exemplar of the Jews. If so, the scholarly presentation of Jesus is not the intellectual act of following an ethical teacher, nor of discovering a predecessor. Rather it seems an act of justifying Reform Judaism in the eyes of the world court (which in the West is Christianity). No non-Western Jew has written at all extensively on Jesus.

Hagner refers to "an obvious natural reluctance among Jewish scholars to admit any uniqueness in Jesus and his teachings" (257). Why this may be so deserves attention. Jews ascribe uniqueness to George Washington, to Thomas Jefferson and, among religious leaders, to the Buddha, Confucius, many mystics, and the Church fathers. This discovery of uniqueness would seem to be natural to a people who boast of a Rabbi Tarfon, "a man of plain common sense," as well as a Rabbi Akiba, a subtle logician (Neusner, 1965, 77-78). We honor Rabbi Gamliel who was stubborn and dictatorial (ibid., 91) as well as Hillel who loved peace and strove to unite his fellow men. And we claim Rabbi Eliezer the Great, who was ultra-conservative, as well as Rabbi Joshua ben Hananya, who was a political rebel (ibid., 97). If Jews do not find uniqueness in Jesus, I suggest it is because he has become a citizen of the world, or precisely because such a claim may denote a reclamation in which Jews do not engage.

On the other hand, Hagner's notes seem to indicate that Jews do recognize a uniqueness in the teaching of Jesus. He quotes Zeitlin questioning whether "turn the other cheek" and related principles would allow society to function (154). He quotes Lapide as saying of the antitheses in the Sermon on the Mount that they "smack of opposition to the Torah and [are] therefore unrabbinic in tone" (101). He quotes Montefiore's statement that Jesus' attitude towards the law "was novel and even revolutionary" (89). He quotes Klausner on Jesus' abrogation of the Sabbath (107); Sandmel on Jesus' repudiation of the food laws (115); and so on. Nor is it the case that Jewish appreciation is all negative. Hagner quotes Montefiore as commending Jesus' intent to seek out and aid the sinner rather than, as the rabbis, waiting for the sinner to "meet you in your sheltered and orderly path..." Montefiore says "that form of love seems lacking" in Judaism, and is "something both great and new" (198-9).

The question of Jesus' originality may indeed need more thought. Two points are cogent here. First, perception of originality is not necessarily exaltation or commendation. Shakespeare was indeed original and praiseworthy but, on the other hand, originality is to be found in people such as Stalin, who was not praiseworthy. For a Jew, Jesus does not compare to either of these extremes. Second, a substantial basis of similarities needs be established before scholars can begin intense criticism without seeming to revert to the previous attitude of hostile criticism and polemical discourse.

Conclusion and Starting Point

Donald Hagner has authored a text which deserves to be read and studied. Not only is it a well-written survey of some leading Jewish opinions on the teachings and person of Jesus, but his penetrating, provocative criticisms deserve close attention. Hagner's statement on the misuse of parallels between Jesus and the Talmud (220ff) ought to be a prod to better scholarship. Further, one should feel the sting reflected in his refrain that the originality of Jesus, supposedly denied by Jewish authors and attributed to the piety of the Church, cannot adequately account for his having become an object of devotion in the Church. Jews should pay more attention to the developing Church and ask how and why Jesus became accepted in such a dignified manner by an alien culture. Christians, on the other hand, ought to ask why Jesus was not accepted by the rabbis, the Judeans, and the extensive diaspora community. At one point, before the activity of interpretation, Jesus was rejected by more than accepted him. For Jews, this is only an interesting historical question. For Christians it is more cunning.

Hagner has said, "the Jesus whom Jewish scholars regard as capable of reconstruction is by definition the Jewish Jesus" (78). We have seen above that Hagner basically agrees with this premise. I have objected to the tiny word "reclamation," but "reconstruction" seems entirely adequate. Hagner goes on to say: "By definition, the Jewish Jesus is the Jesus of history" (ibid.), a sentiment which he finds in tension with the Jewish "moderate-to-strong emphasis on the historical unreliability of the Gospels" (80). His assertion is just.

Are we to say, then, that Jesus was not Jewish? Or that his Jewishness is irrelevant? Or, finally, are we to take an historically agnostic position? Neither of these choices seem appropriate. To a certain extent, concentration on the Jewishness of Jesus, or the alternatives suggested above, smack of childishness. I do not see how one can say of an historical character in a situation similar to that of Jesus that he is "ours" or "theirs." Yet simply not taking a position is not feasible. Jesus predated the rise of Christianity and predated the 70

C.E. transformation of Judaism reflected in the Talmud and other rabbinic sources. One thinks of Karl Marx who, in reference to a political organization of his day announced: "If these are Marxists, I am not a Marxist."

If these are reclamationists, I am not a reclamationist. I have suggested several different motives which may compel a Jew to write about Jesus. These include, but are not limited to: (1) a vehicle for a goodly presentation of Judaism, more specifically, Reform Judaism; (2) an acceptance of a controversial topic for the sake of selling books; (3) a scholarly critical acumen applied to a subject perceived to be of interest; (4) an internal Jewish word of warning or a drawing of lines of demarcations between Jewish culture and Western culture; (5) a true search for amenable understanding in Jewish-Christian dialogue. Reclamation is not an issue for any one of these positions.

I suggest that Jewish authorship is concerned, to one degree or another, with each of the above. What we have at the hands of people from Klausner to Flusser is not a reclamation of Jesus, but an assessment of Judaism; not a profession of respect for Jesus the Jew, but a profusion of regret that Christians have not seen in Jesus the fruits of Judaism. We have in Jesus not a representative of Judaism, but a method for representing Judaism. To misunderstand this fact is to misdirect one's criticism. We cannot, in this manner, promote and advance discussion.

Chapter Nine

Rosenzweigian Meditations on Paganism, Anti-Judaism, The Holocaust, and Rejudaization of the Church

Introduction

The Church is in confusion (see Chapter Six). This is certainly the case in the most visible Church, the Roman Catholic. As a result of the liberal -- or should be say "experimental" -- Pope John XXIII, followed by a series of conservative Popes, the Catholic Church has effectively vanquished the apathy of indifference and silence only to reap a broad spectrum of agendas and programs. In a single Church, individual Catholics are torn between having lost the Latin Mass and not having gained the liberating theology implied in the wide strokes of Vatican II. Theologians battle between substantiating the authority of the Pope and disposing of the position entirely. Whatever else may be said about the Catholic Church, there can be no doubt that she has made astounding strides into the fragmented twentieth century.

The confusion extends to the less visible assemblies of the Church as well. Denominations which are not as highly structured as the Catholic Church are in as much of a wallow. It is increasingly common for a church to abandon its affiliation with one council and petition for entry into another. The United Church of Christ, for example, is composed of different "sects" with diverse agendas and beliefs. This does not prevent these people from living in harmony nor, when the need is felt, of seeking a new harmony. Latin was never a question for these people, but Hebrew is becoming more and more a second language. The Hebrew Scripture has been an important element of the Reformation since Luther, but is becoming ever more a concern now that historical-critical methods have all but demolished the "Christ as an interruption" theology of the last thousand years. The shock of discovering a Jewish Jesus is having an effect on the Church, a discovery which continues, and is slowly finding its way from the scholars to the laity.

If there is a single guiding thread to the confusion of the Church, a single emphasis which seems woven through the various trajectories and interests, it is a new rapprochement to Jews and Judaism. The discovery in Jesus of a Jew who identified with his people and heritage is having an effect. The Jewish Jesus was a pre-Holocaust scholarly investigation initiated by Jews as well as Christians. Isaac M. Wise, Claude Montifiore, Joseph Klausner, and above all Franz Rosenzweig have contributed to the understanding that Jesus was a Jew before the issue became a Christian investigation into the sources.[1] Theirs is a fascinating facet in the history of ideas. Nevertheless, in a certain sense, it was the Holocaust which required of the Church a new approach to the Jews.

The engineers of the Holocaust intended to utterly obliterate the Jewish people, to burn their bodies as well as their books. Thus, the Holocaust was designed to destroy the Jews of the present, the Jews of the future, and the Jews of the past. The fact that the Church came to understand their responsibility in creating the Holocaust by creating and relying on the "teaching of contempt"[2] may have had a number of sources. It may be the case that one of the impulses for studying the Holocaust, anti-Judaism, and antisemitism was concern for how the fact that obliteration of all Jews -- past, present, and future -- would have effected a Christian theology which had largely defined itself over and against the Jews.

Because the Church is a significant element in our common world, Jews are required to respond to the current frustration of the Church. We may hope the current confusion is not debilitating but creative. That this would appear to be the case seems assured by the commitment of certain theologians to penetrate the mysteries of the Jewish people in their covenantal relationship with God as well as their political composition in the world. Jews are being approached as a people in their own right, with their own requirements and agenda. When Jews respond to the Church, however, our response is likely to be as confused as the object of our considerations. We need a guide through the tangle of issues and events.

The problem with our response to this point has been that we have seen no context to respond to other than that which manifested itself in anti-Judaism, antisemitism, and the Holocaust. For an idea to make sense it must be made in a coherent context or, as in this case, a context must be built. Just as it would not make sense for a contemporary American to be sincere about voodoo, witches, or the existence of a devil, so it is the case that it does not yet make sense for a Jew to talk about a committed oneness with Christianity. Alternatively, it does not yet make sense for the typical Christian to talk about rejudaization of his or her faith. It may be the case that the context is being constructed, but we must more fully contend with the constraints. Still, we need a guide.

Franz Rosenzweig

There is no better guide to a Jewish interpretation of Christianity than Rosenzweig. There is, however, at least one significant problem with using Rosenzweig as our guide. This stellar figure in Jewish thought died in December of 1929. He missed, as it were, the Holocaust, the founding of the state of Israel, and the pronouncements of the World Council of Churches and Vatican II. Rosenzweig will have to be pulled through the significance of these three events.

If Rosenzweig were alive -- we may risk the error of speculation, and the even greater error of speculation to an "authority" -- he would be amazed at contemporary Jews. We are horrified but clear about the Holocaust. We are confident about the State of Israel. We are confused about our response and reaction to Christian awareness of Jews and Judaism. Rosenzweig would be distinctly out of place. He was clear about the relations between Jews and Christians (clear in a theological sense, and therefore at a point to which we Jews have not yet advanced) some fifty years before there were what we recognize as Jewish and Christian relations. He was, at best, ambivalent about the Zionist enterprise. Finally, he would have been stunned, and in no sense clear, about the Holocaust. He would have protested that he was a good German citizen, had served in the German army during the war. Rosenzweig must be pulled into our generation.

It was during his service in the German army, as a male nurse -- a healer -- that Rosenzweig wrote The Star of Redemption on scraps of paper which he mailed home from the front. These tiny scraps of paper were woven into a systematic, all-encompassing philosophy of the Jewish and Christian reality (to borrow a phrase from Paul van Buren). I do not intend to briefly introduce his text. It is required reading. I wish only to note some points about the method Rosenzweig used to devise his insights.

In terms of his method, it was programmatically necessary for Rosenzweig to make assertions he did not believe true (or believed true only as a second-level belief). To be sure, he would have thought that because the assertions in question were faith-statements of the Christian community, they were being asserted as "true" for Christians. They were not true for Rosenzweig. We need not be detained by the implications of relativism. Nor is it the case that Rosenzweig would have been disingenuous by asserting things he did not believe true. Rather, the programmatic necessity inherent in what I will call Rosenzweig's "literal dialectic" implied his recognition that every theology is less a statement of fact than a query. Hence, the appearance of "factual statements" is not so much the presentation of absolute truth as a path toward comprehending what one regards as true. In this manner, truths may conflict (or may simply offer alternatives) because they are insightful assertions of perceptions at different stages along life's way. Maturation offers revision of what we previously thought true.

Rosenzweig's "literal dialectic" collapsed two methods into one. In the first place, he took theological assertions (in broad outline) as literally true. His work indicates that he assumed that whatever Jews said about themselves was true and whatever Christians said about themselves was true as well. On the other hand, one of Rosenzweig's greatest achievements was to view the truth of Israel and the truth of the Church as neither conflicting nor collapsing into similarity or unintelligibility. Israel and the Church, after all, make different statements about themselves. If a member of a church made some particular statement about itself, Rosenzweig regarded the assertions as statements of good-faith, as positive self-definitions. If these statements seemed to conflict with assertions the Jewish people made about their own understanding of man, God, and the world, then it must be the case that there is a deeper sense of the others' assertion which will allow it to make sense to both Jews and Christians. Hence, Rosenzweig's fundamental method was a unified program of assessing contrary "facts," taking the faith-statements of each group as literally true, but in a dialectical manner which did not rest content with the literal. In this, Rosenzweig offered an advance over Nietzsche's maddening insight that all truths are "fiction."

The result of Rosenzweig's method was his astounding confirmation that "Jesus is the way." He said: "The Christian dares to enter the presence of the Father only by means of the Son" (Rosenzweig, 1972, 350). This is taken directly from the Christian Bible: "I am the way. ...[N]o one comes to the Father except by me" (John 14:6). Rosenzweig held the statement, in a literal sense, to be true. Yet inasmuch as the statement is not true for the Jew (Rosenzweig says that Jews are *with* the Father and do not need the way, do not need to "come *to* the Father"), the contrasting truths require dialectical thought. This "literal dialectic" is what seems required to develop the Jewish perspective we may expect as a response to the new Christian agenda, an agenda, as suggested, which may be perceived as united around the two core ideas of finding the Jewish roots to Christianity, and adequately responding to the Holocaust.

Church Theologians

The most distinctive idea of Christianity has always been that Jesus of Nazareth was and is the Christ. Nevertheless, not even this most substantive, definitive, faith-statement is exempt from scrutiny. David B. Batstone, a Baptist minister, wrestled with the idea of the messiah in terms of the Holocaust. He quotes Elie Wiesel: "[A] symbol of compassion and love to Christians, the cross has become an instrument of torment and terror to be used against the Jews" (590). This is good rhetoric, and should be appreciated as such. In fact, however, the cross was a Roman means of torture and death. It was used on numerous Jewish citizens as well as other undesirable elements in the Roman empire.

Christianity may be questioned for assuming a poor symbol for love. The cross did not stand for love. The cross stands for the means by which the messiah was murderously released from the bounds of this world (as a preliminary act to his resurrection). If so, the cross is an adequate symbol for the Holocaust. The ambivalence of the cross consists in the fact that it can stand for death as well as resurrection. Attempting to redeem the Christian symbol of the cross as something meaningful in a moral sense after the Holocaust, Batstone implies that he does not recognize the dual function, as it were, of the cross. The cross is ambivalent not just in its ability to symbolize evil (for the Jews) and good (for the Christian) but its ability to symbolize the physical evil of destruction for Jew and non-Jew alike. In these terms, the cross is not ambivalent at all. Rather, the cross merely suggests a Christian hope. Batstone implies a transformation of the symbol which asserts the Christian truth. If the ambivalence of the cross were recognized (the antinomy of good and evil), the rhetoric of symbolism would drastically effect both religions. I do not speculate about the results of recognizing the ambivalence except to say that if the thought were to be maintained consistently, the cross would be forsaken for the image of the oven.

Batstone also quotes Wiesel's charge that "any messiah in whose name men are tortured is a false messiah" (ibid.). Again, good rhetoric is not always good logic. We Jews would not want to claim that cessation of torture in the name of Jesus would make Jesus available to us as a true messiah. In fact, a teacher is not responsible for the operative misunderstandings of his or her students. Intellectual errors may be corrected by reasoning. Programmatic errors are only most difficultly corrected at the same time as the original program is retained. Once a deed is done, it is finished except insofar as it entails consequential deeds. History is a report of done deeds. Theology, on the other hand, is as much an imperative as an assessment. What we see occurring with certain theologians seems more than simple correction of intellectual errors. With the thinkers in question, Christianity is being engaged in a radical investigation into the very program of faith.

In particular, Batstone implies a requirement for Christians to re-think the purpose of Jesus' messiahship and the meaning of his having "rendered ineffective the power of death" (590), that is, the meaning of personal salvation, of our world having been redeemed, and the significance of the return of Christ. The Christian has a significant bit of re-thinking in which to engage. Yet we should be confident that Christianity has engaged in continuous thinking since the first, and her energy has not abated. What Batstone recommends, in fact, is a re-phrasing (a new rhetoric), not a re-doing (a new praxis).

Nevertheless, Batstone was among those pointing the way. He spoke of the Church to be formed "in relation to [Jesus'] messianic life-style instead of emptying the content of his humanity into ontic categories of divine existence" (598). What is at issue, then, is the engagement of rational, critical activity as applied to coherent and creative action which is intended to achieve a goal (a goal we trust will be pursued as a contribution to the creation of "the good life"). What Batstone essayed as important, then, was not theology as an abstract discipline, but as a directive; not as metaphysics, but morals. Batstone expressed this by saying, "the authenticity of our theology is measured by the compassion of our humanity" (599). Heresy, then, will come to be thought of as unreasoned, erroneous behavior, not failure to hold to the official line as expressed by the Church.

Theologians have been awakened to the need for distinction between the abstract and the practical by recognition and assessment of the Holocaust. The fact of Shoah brought not a few theologians to recognize the absurdity of the idea that any punishment received by any Jew anywhere at any time, regardless of circumstance, was just punishment for rejecting the salvation offered by Jesus. Shoah was so overwhelming that it far outweighed the illusion of this world as redeemed, or close to being redeemable. The Holocaust, in a sense, sent the Christian image of Jesus, a Jew, up in flame. What we ought to beware of is that the developing image of the Jew does not become inflammatory.

Paul van Buren has accomplished some remarkable thinking in a manner which may be called, or assumed to contribute to, "rejudaization" of the Church.[3] While many Christians call for Christian theologians to become more familiar with the Hebrew Bible and the rabbinic writings to assess the structure and rhythm of life in Jesus' day, van Buren expresses a concern that the Church needs "to attend to Israel's more recent voices, those of its Rabbis and others, in order to hear them as the Jewish Scriptures" (167). How much more seriously he takes contemporary rabbis than do Jewish lay-people! It is not clear whether he means that the Church should hear Jewish thinkers in a similar manner as they hear the Jewish scriptures, or whether he means the Church ought to hear contemporary Jewish thinkers as "oral Torah." If van Buren means the former, he is concerned with politics in the Church insofar as Jewish interpretations are applicable and corrective to Church politics. If he means the latter, van Buren may be recommending that Christians look upon modern post-Holocaust Jewish thinkers as achieving insights and developing interpretations which are parallel with the inheritance of the prophet. This would suggest contemporary Jewish thinkers are more insightful or intuitive concerning how we ought to think of the "really real" than Christian theologians.

Van Buren says that "Jesus is Israel for the Church... To this day, the church needs that people in order to have Jesus as he is, as a Jew, not a Gentile" (263). Van Buren says, on the one hand, that Jesus represents Israel and, on the other, implies that the people of Israel, the Jews, need to re-present Jesus. Alternatively, Jesus is Israel and Israel is Jesus. The idea of Israel in the Church as Jesus, as the body which is the Church, can be taken in a supersessionist or an integrationist manner. Clearly van Buren does not mean to make the church seem superior by extracting the living people Israel. Just as clearly, however, Israel cannot be so abstractly integrated into the Church as cogent commentators on themes of christological interests.

It is apparent that Jesus, as would be interpreted by a Jewish thinker, is radically different than any interpretation anyone other than the most liberal Christian will permit. Contemporary Jews speak in a rather vague manner, if at all, with regard to Christian theological understandings of Jesus. They do so precisely so as not to seem too negative or intrusive. The following, although not originally a Jewish joke, adequately expresses the Jewish understanding of the basis of Christianity: Easter has been called off; the body has been found. In other words, Jesus was a man. He died. To say anything more than that is to infringe on Christian beliefs. Indeed, to say even that much is to infringe and risk offense. Wiesel, as we have seen, does not speak about Jesus but about the cross. Jesus has done nothing to us or for us. He was a man who sought to reform developing Judaism. The reform is recognized by Jews as accomplished by the rabbinic successors of the Pharisees, or again by the followers of Mendelssohn, or Isaac Wise. Jesus' reform was contrived into a christology, a conviction that salvation was effected for all who would accept Jesus as the one who effected the salvation. Salvation was guaranteed, in other words, for everyone who would agree that salvation was guaranteed. There are two extremely diverse images of Jesus. The Church may need the Jews, but not for definition, or re-presentation of Jesus. They need Jews, perhaps, as critics; as not so disinterested bystanders observing theological reformulations.

A related ambivalence is expressed when van Buren says that the "Gentile church prays in its own proper way when it learns to pray with Israel" (294). Without clarification, van Buren may be taken to mean either that Gentiles have no proper way of their own, or that the way of Israel is the Gentile way, a way to be learned. Either is equally offensive. Alternatively, van Buren may mean that Gentiles need to learn to pray along-side of the Jewish people. If so, this is not something the Church needs Jews to teach them. It may be something the threat of the Holocaust has taught them.

What may elicit Israel's concern, should elicit Jewish cognition of the Christian endeavor, is that Jews and Judaism support Christian service to God. This idea can be expressed in terms more coherent than a Christian "rejudaization." If we bracket, reduce, and eliminate the mea culpa Christianity seems to be experiencing over the Holocaust, what we are left with is recognition by Christian theologians that there is good in the Jews. There is at least more good than is implied in the extermination of vermin. What Christian peoples, not only theologians, ought to do is support and defend, ennoble, enhance and extend any good they perceive. There is, of course, good to be perceived among people the world over, not only Jews. To recognize the good and support it in its otherness would be a positive endeavor, and not psychologically debilitating as implied in the mea culpa.

Judaism is obviously not going to be accepted in any significant sense by Christian people (else they would cease being Christian and start being Jews). The ambivalence expressed by van Buren would serve only to alienate those Christians who would gladly see the Church take a clearer stand on moral issues, but who miss the Latin service, or those who are proud to see the Church confront world historical endeavors on their own terms, but are offended by theologians doing analytic destructions of the Bible. A positive attitude would assume that a majority of Christians would like to have a stable basis of tradition on which to rest, but would like to see these traditions conform to contemporary concerns. This would seem to be the principle behind most reform movements, including the rabbinic, the Enlightenment, and a number of modern reforms. The principle seems to suggest that the apple cart should not be upset all at once. Jews can understand the Christian mea culpa assertions that the Holocaust was an evil in Christian Europe, and may stand in a negative relationship to Christian hermeneutics and typological self-aggrandizement.

Jews understand the Holocaust as having occurred at the expense of the despised and rejected Jew, and may encourage a Christian reinterpretation of the meaning of the events. But the historical shape of Christian exposition is mere background material compared to the more likely fact that the Holocaust was formulated by those who had little Christian spirituality and who read the theologians, if at all, with brutish eyes. It seems more likely that the Holocaust was, in other words, formulated in "Christian Europe" by those we perhaps too self-righteously refer to as 'pagans' who "heard" the silence of Christians and slowly, methodically turned beatings into deportations, slave labor into murder. Yehuda Bauer begins with the fact that "there was no long-range extermination plan" (Bauer, 27). Christianity was in moral error to be silent when denunciation was in order. But only a monster would have understood this silence to be permission for the most "un-messianic-like" behavior: *mass murder*. We do not live in messianic times.

To recognize and support the good in other people seems a worthy endeavor which will contribute to messianic times. Jews will recognize there are good elements in Christian people -- that not every time you scratch a goy will you find an antisemite (but then again, why would we go around scratching goyim?) -- and, with study, will recognize good elements in Christian theology. Yet we will not accept Christianity (else we would cease being Jews). Indeed, we Jews are, once confronted with a significant other, compelled to think Judaism in more acceptable terms. Christians are just as obviously compelled to think their faith in a more coherent manner. It is a psychological necessity we share and can neither of us forsake. Our private need in itself does not prevent either of us from recognizing good in others, and supporting and defending that good in every manner possible whether we understand the genesis, agree with the intention of the phenomena, or not. I have already said that we do recognize good in others. Thus far our "support" seems too limited to commentary concerning how their lifestyle or praxis activity infringes upon our own.

The only way we can take van Buren's remarks seriously is as deliberate overstatements, hyperbolic utterances submitted to correct the extremes of the pendulum by a forceful counter balance. His Rosenzweigian application of over-determining the literal may be fruitfully viewed as both corrective of our past disinterest with one another and as a warning to the Church that "rejudaization" may lead to the demolition of Christianity. The reason for not rejoicing in the demise of Christianity will be made apparent below. For the moment we may say that what we wish to be abolished is not Christianity, nor certainly Christian peoples, but pagan brutality. As the Holocaust indicated, both Jews and Christians have an interest in routing such paganism.

Reactions to the Holocaust

The mea culpa of Christian theologians is inadvertently a matter of pain and frustration of the Christian laity. Too often newspaper editorials carry notice that this or that individual is "tired" of hearing Jews harp on the Holocaust. Dismissive letters to editors are proof that we Jews are not adequately doing our task, which must include explaining that the Holocaust was an irreligious revilement of life, one which effects Christianity as much in theory as it did the Jews in the flesh. Viewing the forms of Christian pain and frustration must make us aware of the fact that Christianity understands itself as a religion of hope and joy (as does Judaism). Indeed, the primary text of Christianity is called the "good news." One aspect of Holocaust education must be to teach the "tired" people that Christianity cannot be a movement of joy, hope, and blessedness unless and until she contributes to the creation of the conditions of blessedness. It is true that many theologians know this to be a fact. The problem is, in part, that the laity is unaware, is at home writing letters to the editor without having read their theologians. As a result, the laity will only hear whispers of guilt and hints of the demise of their faith. They hear the term "rejudaization," and this is bound to cause reaction.

If Christian peoples hesitate over the deplorable course of modern history, the potential loss is immeasurable. There are quite enough infidels in the Western world without adding the newly disillusioned to their ranks. Irreligious pagans are problem enough; disillusioned pagans will trouble us all. Their efforts may not be applied to a Dionysian frenzy, for which they will not be experienced, but to frenzy for the sake of frenzy. It was this, and not Christianity, which we saw grow in Germany in the 1930's. If Christianity is to be indicted it should be because the convictions of the Church did not stand her people in the faith to a degree which would have enabled them to resist heathenism. It is not the negative side of Christian theology which was at faulty -- for we have never in over nineteen-hundred years seen a frenzy such as occurred in Germany -- but the negative evolving without the built-in limits of the positive. The fact that the "religion of love" can have hated throughout its course in the world is deplorable. But aside from beatings and other torments (including death), such hate was not perceived to effect Christianity as it did the Jews. The fact that Jewish people -- any people -- die as a result of hatred is lamentable. The fact that Christian inspired hatred of the Jews showed Christianity not yet the full embodiment as the religion of love must have had some effect on the practitioners of the faith. This effect did not, until our generation, become conscious in a movement of theological insight. No ancient Church father has been cited as an important author who spoke against persecution in the name of religion. Jew-hatred never, until today, required a swing in the pendulum. Nevertheless, the positive elements of Christianity, the literary requirement to love, held the limit to the hatred which was built around intellectual contempt. Christianity provided abundant evidence that hatred existed in literary form, but the same literature called for the practice of love. The fact that this practice was not perfect, again, is evidenced in the literature. The writings did never seem sufficient to recall the faith, never enough to inspire the people to forsake hatred and practice love. Nor were the presumed sub-texts of hatred so overwhelming as to require the people to forsake the religion itself. Thus, although the scorn and derision were preserved, so was the call-back from scorn and derision. What we saw in the 1930's was the absence of the call-back, the absence of Christianity.

We Jews are not overly concerned about the development of Christian theology. We may, of course, offer suggestions and models, but we cannot and will not legislate the guiding principles of a renewal of Christian faith after the Holocaust. What we ought to be concerned about, however, is how use of the term "rejudaization" may affect Jews. We ought be concerned, in other words, about how the term impinges in the current context, when what we Jews and Christians need is a change of context. The issue is not "typical Jewish paranoia" about how something will or will not effect Jews, but what Christian thinkers are proposing to accomplish before the people who, essentially, are to accomplish the proposal are prepared to do so. Christians would seem to run the risk of playing into the current context of negative impingements. The theologians who speak about a rejudaization of Christianity risk three distinct, but related, problems.

In the first place, talk about rejudaization may impact the Jewish self-image. As noted, we do not yet have a context within which it makes sense for us to hear Christians use the term "Jew" in any context suitable for respect, admiration, or beneficial illustration. I do not deny the fact that the contemporary theologians in question are moving in that direction. The problem is that the current context suggests that the Jew is important for Christianity in supersessionist terms, in terms of reprobation, repudiation and repugnance. When theologians in the past spoke of the humiliation and rejection of the Jews, adherents to Judaism did not recognize themselves as the objects of scorn. There is more than sufficient proof that there is a new image of the Jew being spoken into existence. We Jews have an obligation to study the pronouncements of the church as her theologians fight through their part of our shared confusion. We have the additional responsibility of contributing to the new images being devised. There is, in other words, the promise of a new context for the relations between Jews and Christians. But promise is not fulfillment.

In the second place, there is the risk of a "we have done more than our share" mentality. This type of reasoning would be detrimental insofar as it suggests the conversations may be broken off if the other side does not make appreciable strides. Such recriminations are not at all unexpected inasmuch as movement on one issue should require similar movement from the other side. It is not unexpected because it is a fundamental aspect of our accepted psychological make-up (the context of our expectations). Father John Pawlikowski, for example, says: "The new proclamations of bonding and partnership on the part of the churches cannot long endure if they remain a one-way affair with no concomitant declaration from the Jewish side." Pawlikowski is no mean spirited person, nor is he ignorant of the make-up of Judaism. His statement, however, effects a Jewish response. In the present context, such an assertion compels Jews to reject the further reaches of dialogue (theological discussions which are a healthy advancement beyond the mere creation of a context of conventional get-togethers). Given our current dominant psychology, Jews may say, "Look. You do what you think right, but leave us alone. You make your own decision, but do not require that we respond to your decisions." Indeed, the question raised here is whether the theologians are undertaking their re-assessment of Judaism as an aspect in their re-assessment of Christianity, or whether they are doing so for our benefit. If the former, then our participation may be limited to what we feel necessary, and what they are willing to hear. If the latter, then we may wonder what the theologians regard as our benefit. What is to our benefit is achieved by what we think and do as a community. The criticisms and comments of the other may be offered, and should be assessed by us, but we do not thereby relinquish our right to reject the criticisms and comments. This is a plea, then, that Jews and Christians undertake investigation of the other for the purpose of their own (enlightened) self-interest. The first benefit of dialogue ought to be what we learn to appreciate of the other as we make positive assertions about ourselves. If dialogue is anything other than appreciating ourselves more and more, learning to think our traditions and new thoughts in a developing context of appreciating identity in difference, then Jews may not feel compelled to enter into dialogues. Nor might Christians. On the other hand, if dialogue offers a pluralistic way to Jewish reform or Jewish renewal, then dialogue is to be appreciated and sought after. This is not to deny that more and better dialogue is expected in the future.

The third problem concerns the Christian lay self-image discussed briefly above. Thomas Hopko put his finger on this problem when he said "...the anti-Semites are scandalized by the Jewish elements in our faith, rather than inspired by its anti-Jewish teachings" (Hopko, 192).[4] I will not assess the second part of his statement, but Hopko is clearly aware that anything which smacks of Judaism or Jews is repugnant to a certain segment of the Christian population. Again, I am not claiming a "scratch a goy" syndrome, but recognizing that Christianity is thinking its way out of an anti-Judaic matrix which has officially and unofficially incorporated many theologians and lay people. Elements of Christianity which are "Judaic" have had a tenuous existence in the Church. Spiritually, Christians may be Semites -- which is not the same as being "spiritual Jews" -- but the only acceptable Semitic instance allowed for a great portion of the churches is Jesus himself. And he somehow rose above all that.

Batstone says Christian theology "must be rewritten..." (588). I think that is true. But it has always been, and will always be, true. I am concerned, however, that reactionary reverberations will result in the Church if the rewriting of theology occurs largely in reaction to a situation which is, at best, tacitly the fault of the Church. Christianity ought not be in the future, and should not have been in the past, a reaction to any image of the Jew. Rather, Christian theologians must -- and eventually will -- direct their efforts to making their theology a wholly positive substantiation of a principle of discourse which guarantees that theology is recognized as praxis. We Jews, for our part, ought to stand amazed that there is a religious revival going on around us which is both religious and not set against the Jewish people.

The Jewish concern for these problems is not minimized by thinking that they will be argued away by good intentioned people. No doubt there are plenty of good intentioned people in the world -- Batstone, van Buren and Pawlikowski represent Baptists, Episcopalians and Catholics with good intentions. We Jews can appreciate, even admire, their being in the forefront of the development of a new image of the Jew. We can even hope that one day it will become similar to the image we have always held of ourselves -- as diverse yet honorable. What I do not think we can condone is the intertwining of objective assessment of others with the subjective, even emotive, issues of antisemitism and the Holocaust. What I do not think beneficial is a mea culpa beating of the chest so loudly that it drowns out the heart beating within.

Conclusion

My argument is not that individuals claiming to be Christian have not contributed to antisemitism or participated in the Holocaust. They have. People *claiming* to be Christian have gone well beyond tacit acceptance of atrocious behavior. They held the pens which wrote, for example, that Jews are "lustful, rapacious, greedy, perfidious bandits" and "inveterate murderers, destroyers, men possessed by the devil" (quoted in Flannery, 48). They held the pens which recommended the synagogues and Jewish schools be "set fire...and [the faithful should] cover with dirt whatever will not burn, so that no man will ever again see a stone or cinder of them..." (Luther 1). They held the doors to the crematorium. They held them closed! They held the keys to the kingdom. And dropped them!

I would suggest these people are not Christians, or not efficaciously Christian. Of course, similar criticisms can be raised against people who profess to be Jews, yet have never, for example, read Pirke Aboth or Sanhedrin or even the prophets in more than a cursory manner, and therefore do not act on the principles espoused as Judaism. Non-Judaic Jews? Their professions are as little cogent as a sandlot hopeful can truly say he plays for the Yankees or the Dodgers. Further, I argue that Christianity, and Judaism, have more to gain from the development of real Christian behavior than from the mea culpa which merely regrets failure. In other words, Christians ought to stop kvetching about the past and do something about the future. Cannot a similar criticism be levelled against ourselves?

Two questions must be addressed: what is meant by real Christian behavior? And how is doing something about the future to be begun?

Too many people, Christian and non-Christian, refuse to admit the Holocaust occurred. Others, as noted, are quite tired of hearing about the Holocaust. For Jews, the Holocaust has resulted in a perpetual memorial to the victims and the survivors. Holocaust literature has been incorporated in not a few liturgical motifs and merits mention during Passover and Purim, both festivals of terror which issued into deliverance. Ultimately, all Jews were victimized and all survived. Writing and talking about the Holocaust is a means of memorializing victims and survivors. Sequentially, talk about the Holocaust is a means of identifying victims everywhere, and suggests the imperative of ending the conditions of victimization.

For Christians, the Holocaust seems to be becoming a monument and the response a monumentalization. What is needed is not a mea culpa, but a sensitivity concerning what needs to be done to prevent future genocide or victimization in any form, against any people: Jews, Gypsies, Blacks, Cambodians, Pakistanis, Croatians, Somalians, or whomever. In this Jews and Christians share an obligation.

That this imperative is not alien to Christian peoples is clear from the sources themselves. Paul, for example, characterized Christians as people who ought to be concerned with "all that is true, all that is noble, all that is just and pure, all that is lovable and gracious, whatever is excellent and admirable" (Philippians 4:8). In these days long after prophecy has ceased, these virtues are as close as one can come to being prophetic instances of indenture in the world. Hence, they imply a political imperative. They are also virtues which any Jew can ascend to sharing. Such a being cannot possibly be an antisemite, cannot possibly participate in a Holocaust either actively or tacitly. A Christian is a person of conscience and sensitivity. Christians do not require a re-judaization of the Church. Authentic Christianity is sufficiently Judaic (as a reading of the Letter of James may indicate). And if this is the point of the "rejudaizers," then they should be calling for a return to "authentic Christianity," however they will define that term. "Rejudaization," on the other hand, suggests rejection of Jesus. Judaization, Judaism, Jews -- however else these terms may be defined -- include rejection of Jesus. In the present context, any implication of rejection of Jesus implies a required rejection of Jews. "Christians" who live without Jesus are more likely than not brutal pagans. Brutal pagans are fervent for Holocausts. If so, we Jews are in the curious position of defending the man of three births. If so, we hope that Christians can continue to do their slow midrash on his physical birth, his baptismal birth, and his resurrectionary birth.

A related question is whether Christianity has an exclusive relationship with Judaism; finds good only in Judaism, as van Buren occasionally stresses? A few comments of the theologians sound this way. Other theologians evidence a sense of good or worthiness in the Palestinian people, in Buddhists, and so on. Jews have also found good in Gentile authors such as Plato, Aristotle, Shakespeare, etc. There is good in Buddha, Gandhi, Martin Luther King, and many others. Jews have continually assimilated the good from cultures which are not and cannot be Jewish (Aristotle was assimilated and transformed by Maimonides; Jews not only recognized a "Jewish" refrain in King, but learned form him as well). It is important to keep this process effective as a coherent means of rejuvenating Judaism, updating Judaism, reinvigorating Judaism. What is required in Christianity is an update of Christianity, a reinvigoration, and a rejuvenation. To call what is happening before our eyes a re-judaization is unnecessarily restrictive. The term prompts a special relationship to Jews, a unique learning from Judaism. But an exclusive and unique relationship between Jews and Christians is unnecessary as evidenced by the fact that we Jews do not even believe this when, and because, we read Goethe, Desmoulins, Chuang-Tzu, and so on. What might be beneficial would be to compare "a Jewish" perspective on, for example, Confucious with "a Christian" one. What is recommended is a series of considerations which would be welcomed by, and effect, all participants.

Christianity stands as a major bulwark against the conditions which create all forms of prejudice. Christianity has been given the world-historical task of converting all pagans to the way. Christianity has prime responsibility for effacing paganism. The Church performs best when she converts idolatrous selfishness into the body of Christ -- i.e. people who query repentance, seek forgiveness and search after the kingdom. In our days the Church has done much to accept her covenantal responsibility. She is to be praised for her stand against anti-Judaism, antisemitism and anti-humanism. She does this best by espousing and developing what are (wrongly) called Christian virtues.

They are, I assume, the virtues of Jesus the Jew, who, as a Jew, was not dissuaded by theological obfuscations.

Use of the term re-judaization, I have argued, will alienate, not convert, the elements among Christians through whom baptism did not "take." The contemporary Jew-hater will regard "re-judaization" as a "Zionist plot." Yet it is precisely this person who should be addressed by the humanizing theologians who see good in diversity, and who also see wickedness but are not immobilized by it.

When will the term "re-judaization" be appropriate? When the sensitivity engendered by dialogue sparks an agreement to confidently be ourselves while speaking (in a non-inflammatory manner) to those who are not like ourselves. When Jews and Christians think through their own heritage and tradition to identify the resources which promote more than a tacit tolerance and inspire a productive sensitivity. This in turn ought to lead to deeper understanding and, compelled by critical thought, may issue in coherent action. By then, having lived and enlivened Judaism for Jews and Christianity for Christians through rejuvenation, renewal, reinvigoration of our best images in diversity, we may pursue the reverie of hope to a point where there will be no anti-Jewish and no anti-Christian sentiments -- no anti-human sentiments -- and also no need for the term "re-judaization."

Authentic Christianity, as taught by Paul, cannot have been responsible for the Holocaust. When the church re-establishes a grass roots interest in providing and protecting all of humanity, then she will bring herself, and therefore help Jews, beyond what we have been calling paganism. These few years since the declarations of the World Council of Churches and Vatican II, Jews and Christians have only brought together the two contexts of Judaism (in all her guises) and Christianity (with her mea culpa). There has been some movement in each context to adjust to the facing of one to another. Without adequate support, widespread contributory insights, and cogently honest design, Jewish and Christian relations will merely return to a new, higher level face-off. What the most creative and intelligent assessors seem to be working towards is an entirely new context. The idea of a *single* context for Jews and Christians will also allow Jews as Jews and Christians as Christians to form a united front with which to approach the various contexts of other cultures which nurture righteousness. But this *single* context for *both* Judaism and Christianity does not require we use each others language, think each others thoughts, or otherwise do other than we do when we are being our authentic selves. Indeed, it may be the case that using identical speech and thinking each others thoughts will cause a similarity from which we cannot learn, for one only learns from otherness. What is required, it seems, is that we each investigate our "authentic sources" and bring authenticity into our quest for heaven, both on earth and elsewhere.

To simply merit heaven is not enough. The righteous need to coherently bond as a united front against contemporary paganism, Hitlerism, exploitation, manipulation and behavior we determine to be "un-godly." I end on a Rosenzweigian note: One cannot simply say, "I am an anti-totalitarian." One must make clear the significance of the depth of his or her anti-totalitarianism, anti-monism, anti-monolithicalism. Each of these "evils" is a hierarchy: totalism is a hierarchy. To deny the hierarchy of totalism and defend the pluralism of oneness is the goal. Achieving the goal requires diverse means. The one is expressed in a variety of ways. The goal is the essential unity of the ways. Oneness will vanquish totalism. Our task is to create the conditions of oneness.

It may be the case that Christianity has developed, more than is suggested by my concerns, a context to say there is a re-judaization of the Church. There is not yet a context for Jews to hear that there is a re-judaization of the Church. It seems part of the reason is that Christian re-judaization looks back, through the Holocaust, to Jesus. Jewish vision is committed to the future. Further, Jews may be afraid that if Christianity looks back far enough, Jesus will be overlooked. If this ever turns out to be the case, re-judaization will be a catch-phrase for that which the early Church fathers demeaned as "judaizing." St. Ignatius in his letter to the Philadelphians said, "Now, if anyone preaches Judaism to you, pay no attention to him. For it is better to hear about Christianity from one of the circumcision than Judaism from a Gentile" (quoted in Richardson, 109). Who will be blamed if "re-judaization" is perceived as "judaizing?"

NOTES

1. The point of referring to these "ancient" authors is not primarily to indicate the sources of our perspectives -- which are very much older -- but to indicate that there was creative thought on the part of Jews, an attempt at creating a new context for discussion, well before the Holocaust, Israel, and positive-tending statements about Judaism.

2. This term was popularized by Edward H. Flannery, a Catholic priest, in The Anguish of the Jews.

3. The following quotes are from van Buren's A Christian Theology of the People Israel. His study of Jesus in particular occurs in Christ in Context.

4. It should be noted that Hopko was not responding to the paper by Father Pawlikowski cited above.

Chapter 10

Noahide Laws, Christian Covenants and Jewish Expectations

Review

Jewish-Christian Dialogue: A Jewish Justification (Novak 1989) is a fitful feast of reasoned assessment designed to advance the essential dialogue between Jews and Christians. David Novak begins with an analysis of the rabbinic designation of the Noahide Laws and traces the cognitive development of relations between Jews and Christians at least to Franz Rosenzweig. In the course of his investigation, Novak presents many insightful points ultimately concerned with the question of how we Jews think about our place in the world.

The primary question of the dialogue between Jews and Christians is announced as "a radical research into the sources of Jewish tradition" to supply the Jewish justification for dialogue as an "empathetic analysis of the Christian partner" (23-4). Novak repeatedly asserts his interest in discovering whether the thoughts of our predecessors might be taken as a model for dialogue "in the present and for the future" (128, passim). Dialogue in this text is characterized as "a desideratum" (14), a possibility, not a fact.

Novak points out that in spite of the voluminous rabbinic and post-rabbinic literature on non-Jews, the Medieval sages were required to view the Christianity of their day "in a different light if Jewish economic relations with Christians were to be justified by Jewish law." Christians had to be viewed as "something other than idolaters, and Christianity itself had to be considered something other than idolatry" (44).

Novak does not justify the dialogue in terms of what conversation between Jews and Christians may do for each of us, except to say that our common enemy, secularism, requires we stand together against the positivist assumptions of our age. Novak says "the predominantly secular civilization is a threat to both Judaism and Christianity... A common threat has created a new common situation." Hence it is not the case that mere economic determinants have made it necessary that Jews and Christians relate. Rather, we are in a *NEW* situation where economic determinants are regarded as a mere fact of life, and the particular religious concerns of both Jews and Christians are required to be enacted in a way rarely before known among us. We are to be religious in the world.

Other than the common enemy, secularism, justifying a united Jewish-Christian front, Novak's Jewish justification is limited to viewing the impediments to dialogue deduced from Jewish intellectual history. Novak begins with, and maintains, the Judaic distinction between Jews and the "sons of Noah." He deftly traces modifications of the theme of the Jewish relationship with Christians through the thoughts of Rabbenu Jacob Tam, Rabbi Menachem Ha-Meirri, Maimonides, Rabbi Jacob Emden, Hermann Cohen, Martin Buber, and Franz Rosenzweig. Both Novak and most, but not all, Jewish thinkers have retained the image of Christianity as falling under the commandments pertaining to the Noahides. This has been the case even when Christians were viewed as constituting a community superior to the pagans who legitimately are to be regarded as "sons of Noah."

Novak believes a "radical change in history has taken place" (4). Traditional Jews have not, since R. Menachem Meirri in the 14th century, understood that "Christians (and Muslims) were in another category altogether from the ancient idolaters mentioned in Scripture and the Talmud and, therefore a different Jewish view of them had to be formed" (ibid.). Novak has adequately stated the fundamental shibboleth from the Jewish side. The dialogue which must now be developed must presuppose "a true mutuality based on a duality that is not to be overcome in the process of dialogue itself" (129). Jews ought to be free to act as Jews, and Christians ought to be free to act as Christians. Neither should be inhibited by the *imagined* expectations of the other, nor should either be limited by the very real influences of secularism. Further, Jews ought to be supported in their Judaism and Christians be supported in their Christianity. Such support is the only genuine method of making our expectation explicit. Our expectation is nothing more, nor less, than helping the other see and act on their covenantal relationship with God and toward all fellow humans. Only with the duality of Jew (as Jew) speaking with Christian (as Christian) can a true mutuality be effected.

Successful dialogue does not require I limit my Judaism, nor the Christian limit his or her Christianity. We each extend our knowledge and understanding in relation with the other. This does not mean we automatically accept the other, nor automatically reject the other. What it means is that we see the alternatives of the other and therefore better define what we believe and why, and modify our behavior in both a rational, creative way, toward the other. The alternative, as we have too often seen, has been a competition of feigned superiority which denies the efficacious behavior of those Jews and Christians who know that such competition is senseless in a world where God is Master of the Universe. If Christians stand in a relationship with God, then our conversation with Christians might well be constructed on the basis of support, friendly criticism, and knowledge that nothing happens without the direction of God.

A dialogue in these terms will allow maximum authenticity for both Jew and Christian. Novak argues that authenticity must avoid the triad of triumphalism, relativism, and syncretism (see Novak's excellent discussion, 14-22). When both Judaism and Christianity are understood as "part of that larger background for the other" (115) each will "constitute the integrity of the other community and not lose the integrity of their own" (19). The integrity will be all the greater when the Muslim community is taken out of parentheses as well.

Novak intends that Jews and Christians behave differently toward one another; behave, in fact, as if the reign of God were a fact in their daily lives. Jews and Christians should behave as if they believe the principles each profess.

Exposition

Jews and Christians have reached a stage where it is morally and spiritually essential that we devise amenable relations. This is the most forceful point to be derived from Novak's book. Novak clearly implies that the medieval basis of economic relations is simply not an adequate foundation for the impending dialogue. He also suggests that relations to this point, however advanced and noteworthy, have simply not been as responsible as each may wish. To achieve greater relations, Jews may have certain expectations of Christians and Christianity, and Christians may have certain expectations of Jews and Judaism. In the Western World, the two are virtually alone in asserting religious ways of life which exist for the betterment of both individuals and the extended community.

Novak says the Jewish-Christian dialogue is important not only for the relations between Jews and Christians, but "the future of all humankind." Both Judaism and Christianity, he continues, "must be able to constitute a role for humanity as a whole, and it must be able to do so more compellingly than secularism" (13). Each of our traditions have asserted, in various explicit and implicit ways, that our diverse perspectives and ways of life are most beneficial for humanity as a whole. Each has asserted superiority in terms of relationship with God and possession of a "program" for achieving just relations (economic, social, political, intellectual, psychological, and emotional). In terms of backing up our claims, then, we each have been, and continue to be, miserable failures. Novak states that we "cannot simply return to our respective covenants for an immediate alternative to secularist universalism" because these covenants are currently constituted and enacted as particularistic (ibid.). The dialogue for which Novak is hopeful, then, has universalistic, messianic overtones.

The new task of the Jews, according to Novak, "is to see how Christians stands before me against the wider background of the world" (115). Novak proposes we Jews no longer view the world as divided into a few of us and a great multitude of others. He suggests we no longer view the world as composed of one evil background against which we stand alone. Rather, the world should be viewed in a more dynamic manner. Christians stand out against the bland and vague multitude. If we achieve the perspective which Novak recommends, we Jews will no longer suffer under the burden of standing alone. "Something" makes the Christian religion different than the vast majority whom we may call "pagan." A new perspective will allow us to see that Christianity can be more beneficial than not.

The Noahide Laws have long been identified as those minimum requirements all pagans were expected to follow. The Noahides, however, cannot be considered our "background" in Novak's sense because pagans do not merit being considered in a foreground in their own right. Being a foreground in Novak's sense means to have a spiritual/religious relationship with God. Pagans constitute the underground of not-yet-spiritual relationship. They are, in fact, groundless. If so, Novak does not merely suggest we return to the medieval Jewish perspective of Christianity as outstanding "sons of Noah." Rather, Christians are different than the Noahides. This is so in spite of the fact, as we shall see below, that Novak structures his analysis on the assumption that Christianity is indeed Noahide.

It should be noted that in contemporary times, when we are not comfortable speaking about pagans, the world is yet conceptualized as divided into us and them. In the Jewish case, however, the 'them' is frequently the great multitudes of Christians. This is the case even when Jews use the term pagan to describe the most horrendous outburst of evil in our century. The Holocaust is too frequently referred to as the results of Christian intellectual or theological history, or the consequences of Christians not performing in a moral manner. These two rationales should be viewed together. If the Holocaust occurred because Christianity failed, then the destruction of Jews can in no sense be blamed on Christianity. On the other hand, if there were or are elements in Christian thinking which inhibit our mutual advance towards the good life, the life God intended we share, then this is evidence that at least some of what Christians announce as theological truth is in fact residue from the pagan past and should be expunged. If Christians are no different than the Noahide pagans, we have no right for such an intellectual expurgation. If Christianity is merely another among the multitudes, we have no implicit rules for treating Christianity any differently than the other nations. If Christianity is not superior to the seven Noahide Laws, which are the *minimum* requirements for all people, we have no redress with regard to violations of the higher and more important moral rules which the nations did and do violate. If Christianity does not transcend the minimum, we have one less ally in the construction of the kingdom worthy of calling God their King.

If Christians are mere Noahides, we have a right to expect only seven actions on their part. Of the seven Noahide commandments, one requires the Noahides establish courts of law, two require they refrain from behavior offensive to God (idolatry and blasphemy), and three require they refrain from particular actions (not to shed blood, not to rob, and not to eat a limb torn from a living animal). Not one of the seven Noahide commandments, with the possible exception of the first (which is limited in intention), requires specific actions be undertaken in a positive direction toward another. The command to establish court is in effect to ask pagans to redress wrongs which have been done, which is a different request than asking them to legislate laws which would prevent erroneous behavior. Once Torah had been written -- and, of course, Jews believe Torah was before the creation of the word -- pagans cannot have devised a cogent positive law. The fundamental negativity of the first Noahide injunction should be compared with the positive direction given in the Ten Commandments ("Remember," "Honor") which Jews and Christians share. In addition, Jews and Christians have developed both extensive commentary and an intensive understanding of what each community is expected to do.

We might imagine our relationship with pagans would be distinct from our relationship with people who claim to have a relationship with God. We might avoid pagans because they were/are oppressive, manipulative, and ignorant. We may, on the other hand, relate in such a manner to expose and correct their ignorance and insensitivity. This "educative" behavior may occur as an act of attempting to convert the pagan, which the pagan might resist as our own expression of showing ontological superiority in our knowledge and worship of God. While it is true we may evidence a kind of superiority to Christians, it cannot legitimately be the ontological superiority of being the only people who have a relationship with God. Further, while it is true that Christians have acted aggressively, oppressively, and ignorantly, their fundamental charge has been to be helpful, submissive to God, and wise as serpents. Novak expresses an equality of this nature when he says both Jews and Christians "are themselves grounded originally and irrevocably in revelatory events" (124). Finally, Jews have historically not sought to convert Christians. Hence, the facts that Christians and Jews have continually related differently than Jews and pagans, that Jews have recognized (if not fully supported) the Christian relationship with God, and do recognize the commandments of a higher morality than the minimum, require we see Christianity differently than we do the Noahides.

Both Judaism and Christianity are constituted on the basis of a whole-hearted relationship with God. This is so even if Jews too frequently emphasize their human responsibilities in such a way that earthly justice seems the prime value, or Christians emphasize a not-yet-earthly spirituality. In fact, both Jews and Christians relate to God on the basis of what each may refer to as 'intentionality.' In true religion, the spiritual is an integral fact of earthly justice, and earthly justice is an aspect of the spiritual. Efficacious inwardness requires construction of a world which will permit an economy and psychology which would remove the impediments to a true individuality in communal relationship under God. I assume thoughts such as these would ultimately elucidate the biblicism common to Jews and Christians. If so, the most subtle enmity between Jews and Christians needs to be removed, and the enmity between religious people and pagans needs be abolished as well.

We have a right to expect much more from Christianity than we do from pagans. Our expectation derives from the fact that Christians are constituted in a manner which announces that they can and will do more with respect to God and other people than was expected of pagans. For far too long the relationship between Jews and Christians has been founded on the basis of identification of the failures of each. Our relationship is indeed futurial in the sense that each of our traditions hold that we ought to "messianically" help, not hinder or ignore, the other. If so, the conception of Christianity as a limited Noahide community inhibits our mutual development toward the worthy goal Novak has identified.

Novak's own retention of the essential Noahide structure of Christianity is summed up in his assertion that the Jewish perspective of Christianity "is based on the question whether Christians are faithful to that aspect of the Law that the rabbis took to be binding on all humanity" (16). He says further, "treatment of relations with non-Jews must turn to the rabbinic doctrine of the Seven Noahide Laws, the basic moral rules the rabbis saw as binding on all the 'children of Noah,' that is, on all humanity" (24). The purpose of relying on the rabbinic designations seems to prevent a "free lance" determination of the relationship between Judaism and Christianity and to maintain the integrity of our tradition. Certainly we cannot invent a relationship! Yet strict adherence to the notion of Christianity as Noahidic inhibits not only our full recognition of the changed status of religions in the contemporary secular world but also the fact that Christianity is continually developing in various aspects as a covenanted religion. From another point of view, we ought to be able to trust our healthy tradition to forge an extended relationship on the basis of inherent optimism as well as reliance on the helpful God.

By identifying the Noahide Laws as primarily a rabbinic doctrine rather than a biblical covenant, Novak allows the following suggestions. First, he implies that the Noahide rules do not have the absolute authority they would have had if they were scriptural rather than rabbinic. Second, he implicitly distinguishes between rules which are accepted by a people and those which are saddled upon an unwilling population (viz., the Noahide injunction against idolatry and blasphemy, which cannot be assumed to have been acceptable to all pagans). Finally, Novak implicitly distinguishes between those who participate in a covenantal relationship with God (among whom we count Jews, Christians and Muslims) and those who, again, cannot be assumed to have a relationship with, and who do not evidence a knowledge of, God.

As rabbinic injunctions, the Noahide Laws are subject to debate, modification, and possible rejection. For purposes of equality, dignity, authenticity, and mutuality, there is merit when we insist upon a distinction between the uncovenanted children of Noah and the covenanted Christians. There is both a moral and an ontological sense in re-asserting that Christians have, and should live up to, their convenanted relationship with God. We Jews should also accept similar moral and ontological promptings from a people who are becoming friends along the way, and are no longer violently hostile critics bent on our disappearance.

I have not personally known any ancient pagans. Nevertheless, I imagine they did not heed the Noahide injunctions against idolatry. If so, they were more than un-biblical; they were immoral. Indeed, rabbinic commentary continually downgraded the nations which surrounded the Jewish nation precisely on this score. Perhaps this is the reason Novak identified the Noahide Laws with rabbinic authority rather than scriptural authority. If the Noahide Laws were biblical, then there should have been intention on the part of all believers to enforce the Noahide Laws as possessing the power divine of commandments. Such an injunction to hostility would have been inadvisable for the small Jewish nation surrounded by idol-worshipping pagans. Jews may shout rules and regulations at other Jews and, if the terms of my argument are correct, we have some obligation to quote Christian moral injunctions to people who want to be Christians -- to advise and accept advice, not to bludgeon and antagonize. No such relationship can have existed between believers and pagans.

In these terms, Jews have a right and an obligation to insist that Christians be Christians, which is to do more than tacitly recognizing the fact. Christians have the same right and obligation toward Jews. If we do develop the mutual respect which attends the ecumenical, the religious, thrust of fulfilling God's intentions for the relationship of one human toward another, then Jews will know they benefit when Christians live as Christians and Christians will know they benefit when Jews live as Jews. The benefit seems to be more obviously religious than might be the case if Jews and Christians come together only to confront a common secularist enemy. It is a regrettable possibility that victory over secularism (whatever that means!) will lead to renewed hostility between Judaism and Christianity.

If, on the other hand, amicable relationship is designed, established, followed and heard as the commandment of God, at least four results will follow. Jews and Christians, by living their beliefs, will engender respect for themselves by continually proving that, first, one being or principle *does* influence moral behavior. Second, proof will be offered that *either* Judaism or Christianity is morally superior to both paganism and secularism.   Third, the operative truth that disagreements are inevitable will be modified by the agreeable behavior which proves that the hope of agreements are more significant. Further, the process of reasoned discussion will allow new responses for changed times. Reasonable and creative solutions will be noted to be more readily forthcoming when disagreements are not only not primary, but are enterprised as a form of dignity in diversity; a form of two, or more, peoples seeking for solutions which are known to effect everyone. Finally, just as Hillel and Shammai, the Pharisees, and Sadducees, Rationalists and Kabbalists might exists under the rubric of *avodah yisroel*, so might all dignity of diverse peoples be understood under the auspices of *avodah adam*. One community might act as a *midrash* for the improvement of the other community and, eventually, all of humankind.

One looks upon the strides made between ecumenical offices of the Catholic Church, the World Council of Churches and various Jewish agencies and hopes for a future which allows Jews to become better Jews while designing a world worthy of participation with those who are not, and need not become, Jews. The non-Jews who are considered morally superior -- called "righteous Gentiles" by the rabbis -- ought to be identified with Christian peoples and distinguished from pagans. We should, however, be aware of another population in western civilization who may be righteous yet neither Jews nor Christians. Albert Camus and Mahatma Gandhi come to mind. It does not seems advisable to identify even the self-professed "pagan" Camus as a secularist. His was simply a different, non-idolatrous, religion which concentrated on human beings in secular society.

Undoubtedly a great impediment to establishing a better relationship between Jews and Christians has been the antisemitism of the Church. I have already argued that the extreme antisemitism which resulted in the Holocaust cannot be deemed a Christian phenomenon. The antisemitism of the Church seems a convenient memory for finding a scapegoat, for giving free reign to any unexpunged pagan feelings of anarchy, chaos, violence. Un-Christian behavior, such as antisemitism, is a means for people who find themselves born Christians to deny the difficult covenant implied in Jesus' ministry. We Jews should not allow historic antisemitism to become a convenient means for rejecting individual Christians, nor ignoring the world's need for Christianity. In the terms I have been attempting to develop, each time a non-Jew establishes a true relationship with God, one of moral and spiritual responsibility, a covenant above and beyond the Noahide injunctions is re-established, the Church is re-born. We Jews say that each time a teaching is repeated in a rabbis' name, the sage's lips move in the grave. We might say, although this is not our terminology, that every time a Christian is purged of paganism, their Christ is resurrected.

I hope to have suggested that the Noahide Laws are not a covenant, and may be radically improved upon. Jews live a covenant which can neither be improved upon, nor should be left behind. An identical statement may be made by Christian peoples. This is not to say that individuals may not improve through their acceptance of tradition, nor that traditions themselves may not be extended. Obviously individuals can deepen their religiosity and cultures can develop new intensities and applications of their core truths. The advantage of recognizing and supporting the moral and spiritual force of the Christian covenant for Christians seems obviously beneficial for both Jews and Christians. One imagines a day when the more Christians exist in the world, the less room there will be for pagan errors and evils.

Chapter 11

A Note on the Friends of Israel and the Jews

Emil Fackenheim says, "the most shocking phenomenon of all concerns those people who forever keep repeating that Israel has a right to exist, and who in saying this legitimate those who say the opposite or act on it" (Fackenheim, 1987, 283). This statement may be true if someone initiated the conversation by saying Israel had a right to exist; if, that is, the assertion was made without a context. If I offer the suggestion "X," I invite the suggestion "not-X."

In a world operating under the principle of fair play, if I offer an opinion I think legitimate I, in a sense, legitimatize the opinion of others (even if they disagree with me). If my assertion is a response to them, on the other hand, I do not legitimatize their opinion with my contrary opinion. I deny it.

Fackenheim continued with the rhetorical question: "What would anyone think of a person who got up and said 'Canada has a right to exist!'"

Here again, if someone simply stood and announced that Canada had a right to exist, we may look at that person and wonder to ourselves if all his or her faculties were functioning properly. Yet the remark that Israel or Canada have a right to exist does not typically occur without a definitive context. Let us propose a context for Canada.

Atomic bombs have been, God forbid, traded between the United States and the hitherto unheard of nation of Iqycrehe.[1] The United States military and civilian population is so dispersed or demoralized that troops sympathetic to the Iqycrehians are able to boat into Florida, lay siege to Washington and neutralize New York. War being an aggressive and expansive phenomena, the Iqycrehians and their lackeys begin to plot against Canada.

For her own part, Canada has not yet committed troops to the war effort. The blitz on her southern neighbor was so swift and unexpected that the Canadians, like the Americans and her allies overseas, were caught totally unprepared. This, in fact, has worked to Canada's advantage. She is neither pre-defeated nor demoralized. Pushing back the rude attack which now begins, her battle is courageous, but allied forces, such as they are, have been committed elsewhere. Canada is relatively defenseless. Her doom is imminent.

The parable being presented can be completed by hypothesizing hostile troops invading from the north and east. Canada is under siege on all sides. In this situation -- in context -- the person who stands and says, "Canada has a right to exist!" is indeed a moral individual, a courageous human being, even a wise person.

We Jews have a word for someone who is an individual (with private opinions) as well as a human being (with public confidence and sympathy) as well as a person (a personable being). We assume such a being -- a human being in the most definitive portrayal -- is, along with other characteristics, wise, intelligent, smart, courageous, active, committed, responsible, a doer, a leader, a moral human being. He or she is a mensch. I have assumed, and think the majority of Jews assume, that any individual person who stands up for Israel and/or the Jewish people is a *mensch*.

Consider: the United Nations is today frequently called the "effective world center of antisemitism."[2] Newspapers too frequently blur the facts in order to create or expand a story of an underdog. Typical conversation on street corners refers to "jewing me" or (on "scholarly" street corners) "pharasaic hypocrisy" (which is apparently a unique behavior associated only with the Jews), hymie-town, and so on. The charge that Jews are "Christ-Killers" is not as infrequent as we would like to believe. The "jew" is a term for everything bad. I once heard a merchandise manager, referring to a bad purchase which required a price adjustment, say, "Let's get rid of this jew." At first, I thought he meant me!

In short, the media and her opposite, politics, hybridize the term "Jew" and "Israel." Do these two terms not designate the same phenomena to a stereotypic mind? The devil incarnate? Again, every support system common to politics and communication serves to reinforce ancient ideas of the Jew and the nation of Israel as a manifestation of that illusory phenomena saddled on the Jew in the name of antisemitism. Between the cracks of the not-always-so-silent pressure to distrust and dislike the Jew, Judaism, Israel (the individual, the religion, the nation, the idea, the corporate entity) is there perhaps not one or two people who ought to be applauded and commended as mensches?

The fact is, Jews are still a minority. Of course, we are a highly organized minority. Yet inasmuch as our systematic approaches to public issues (systematic, perhaps, but by no means synthesized) are themselves a public system, the secret of our success in social and political issues cannot remain secret for long. This is especially the case if we, as we do, brag about our organizational skills. Consider: in the last eight years we have, on not an insignificantly few occasions, been out-maneuvered. From certain technologies having been sold to the Saudis, to Presidents visiting Bitburg, to Papal audiences, we have been out-maneuvered.

Yet considering these meetings, it would seem we would have achieved more mileage, good will, and "points" by exhibiting the meeting with Waldheim, for example, as one between east and west, good and bad. We could have established the terms of a hopeful dialectic. We could have proven our understanding of the Papacy as a political instrument, and understood that the person who sits in that chair has political as well as moral responsibilities. We could have refused to imply that the Pope and Waldheim had something in common. We could have admitted that we cannot have anticipated what the Pope would have said, behind closed doors, to Waldheim. He may, for all we know, have said, "Schmuck, resign!" We could have done a lot better than allow braggarts and loudmouths -- from both the Jewish and Catholic side of the debate -- to feed the press for manipulation.

Since Waldheim visited the Pope as the President of Austria -- very nearly a command performance for a self-professing Catholic "dignitary," but extremely common for non-Catholic leaders as well -- the charge that the meeting condoned and legitimized German war crimes against the Jews was ridiculous. Even if promotion of racism and antisemitism had been on the agenda of Waldheim, he could have been made short work of in the Jewish press for an absurd intention being directed toward the Papal head-of-state. The Pope is responsible, in the latter half of the twentieth century, for promoting Jewish-

Christian dialogue and expunging prejudice and hatred from at least his own people's conscience.

I personally focused on the fact that Waldheim did not deny there was wrongdoing and atrocities committed during the war. He denied only that he participated in any wrongdoing. These are clearly two different claims. As to the veracity of the second claim I am unable to judge. I do know that the United States had barred Waldheim from entering the country, and I assume they had good reason for doing so. Further, I have seen the pictures of Waldheim in his German uniform, which was repugnant, but unfortunately common during the war.[3] In any case, Waldheim seemed to have claimed he did not want to be associated with the atrocities which occurred. (His behavior as General-Secretary of the United Nations is a separate, if related, issue.) His implicit disassociation from the Nazi killing-machine would seem to have been more beneficial for us to have kept in mind during his meeting with the Pope. Not only would we have gained mileage from giving "the benefit of doubt," but would have allowed Waldheim to hang himself, in a figurative manner, if and when definitive proof of his Nazi involvement was released.

Obviously, my point speaks more to our relationship with the Pope than with Waldheim. The benefit of doubt ought always be extended to people who claim to be friends of Israel and/or the Jews. I would have thought this would have been obvious were it not for the outcry of attack against the Catholic Church -- the Church of the Ecumenical Council, the Church of the American Bishops, the Church of new insight and new search for truth in relationship. (Granted, this is also the Church of the failure to write or issue a statement of recognition of the State of Israel. We may try to assess this failure in terms of her concern for Christian citizens in Arab lands. We may also attempt to see a start in this direction with the recognition of the "people of Israel," and so on. It is, nevertheless, a failure).

As for legitimate voices of prejudice, of racism and antisemitism (of which, it appears, Waldheim was such a voice), our attitude should continue to be indefatigable. We should maintain a strict and disciplined commitment to decisions based upon issues of right, not malice. We should be committed to the cessation of every manifestation of bigotry, insensitivity, enmity, apartheid and moral, physical or intellectual suppression that exists. We should be consistent in our stand against stupidity. By and large, I believe we are consistent. If we falter, it is in two regards: first, that we occasionally promote our own "Jewish" objections to antisemitism as if over and against other forms and manifestations of racism; second, we do not always consciously present antisemitism as a factor which maintains vestiges of hatred in other forms.

This is a hazard which we share, for example, with the black freedom fighter, the human rights observer and other minorities. Obviously our own concerns ought to come first. Not only do we know these concerns better, and can speak more cogently about them, but we know them better precisely because we are victims. My only point here is that victimization is a random, yet common, phenomenon -- and it is in our best interest to promote the end to the facilities which promote any and every type of hatred and insensitivity.

Lest my comments make me seem soft against antisemites, racists, bigots and other detrimentally insensitive people, I offer the following comment.[4] We owe a debt of gratitude to those among us who find traces of prejudice in the most seemingly unrelated gesture or word. In spite of their apparently narrow perspective, these people are guardians of culture; not only their own, but every form of culture which might have been and may yet be. No one who genuinely despises unreasoned hatred and bigotry can ever burn a book, even if the book in question argues against their own position or their own people. Would that we lived in a society, in a world, where prejudices were so far behind us that people who find bigotry everywhere did not have a function. We do not. Until we do -- until such a world evolves at our own insistence -- these people alert us to the most insidious traces of that which must be eradicated. We need these people!

We need the black preacher who finds bigotry in the most innocent remark. We will continue to need him or her until innocent remarks are indeed innocent and pure. We need the "bleeding-heart liberal" who discovers violations of human rights in the most abstract crevices. We will continue to need him or her until liberty and justice flow like honey from the mountain. We need the conservative who will find unreasonable foolishness in all phenomena which is not "conservativistic." We will continue to need him or her until all "oppositionary" remarks are neither unreasoned nor foolish. And we need the Jew who continues to find antisemitism in the most naive visits to locations far away, the most vague references in scholarly texts, the most unintentional remark. And we will continue to need him or her until every vestige of prejudice or insensitivity is immobilized, eradicated, forgotten, and gone beyond.

Our common odyssey toward tolerance and mutual respect must be guided by realism, an objective assessment of how things really are in the world. At the same time, our quest for a more suitable existence must be modified by the respect necessitated by sincere difference, and the free giving of the benefit of our doubt. Realism, in other words, ought to qualify both our doubts and our convictions. In truth, we need to sponsor friends of the Jewish people the world around, and fill them with the convictions of the righteousness of our causes. We do not do this by publicly criticizing those among the nations who virtually stand alone, and proud, as making progress towards the end of racial or religious viciousness.

In this paper I have presented two examples of Jews risking the perception, that we are willing to chew off our own hand. The one involved an abstract assessment by one of our greatest living philosophers; the second a public outcry by our most vocal and respected leaders.

Emil Fackenheim has, more than anyone else has shown capable, effectively placed the Holocaust in the forefront of philosophical analysis.   Lest this seem an insignificant or disingenuous accomplishment, all the history, statistics and documentation in the world cannot help us penetrate the atrocity of the crime. Fackenheim himself frequently says the evil is beyond comprehension. Nevertheless, he has provided the analytic tools as well as the dialectical terminology necessary if our insights and concern are to grow more deeply and reasonably away from the staggering inability to comprehend.

If the statement we have been investigating is found to be excessive, it may be because our teacher had momentarily left the calm of study - - which he would, I am sure, argue is necessary (as one would step out of Plato's cave to see the light of day, but then return) -- left to be influenced by the hustle-bustle of quick-lipped, hurried decision, rapid action.   We should be, forgive me, far enough away from the Holocaust that we can at least recognize those non-Jews who also think it atrocious.

I have argued that we should cherish our friends at the same time as we recognize they have different agendas than our own. I trust we can respect their programs if they follow a coherent principle of thought and deed which does not intrude on the actions and thoughts of others. I would go a step further. It is in the best interest of the Jews to cultivate friends, and boast of phenomena in a manner which is in the best interest of the Jews. We ought, in other words, offer the most positive interpretation of borderline, even doubtful events. This should not prevent us from being aware of, and militantly against, insidious prejudices, subtle offenses and all forms of ignorance and brutality. In this manner we maximize the ranks of those who may be willing to stand up for Israel or the Jews. In this manner, we make a clear vocal, moral, and active distinction between the purely evil and all that which is tending toward the good. The good needs help.

If we assume the best intentions, until shown differently, and submit our arguments to the world community stating why our own assumptions are correct, we may persuade the borderline cases to transform themselves into mensches. If we proceed in this manner, we will show a graciousness which the less than gracious -- as well as some who are truly our friends, or would like to be friends -- currently perceive as our failing.

The Book of Proverbs announces: "A soft response turns away anger, but a sharp word makes tempers hot." This penetration of human psychology can neither be improved upon nor gone beyond. We must not fall below the imperatives for progress. Another version of the same truth may be stated thus: *menschhood* follows *menschhood*.

With particular regard to Jewish-Christian relations, the "professional" Jewish attitude does certainly not seem to offer the benefit of doubt. Our ultimate concern, however, cannot be to look for primary antisemitism. We post-Holocaust Jews have an obvious interest in the growing Christian consciousness of Judaism. We live in an era which has made, and continues to make, progress away from a general pagan commitment to the notion that there are too many Jews, or that a single Jew was too many. Our interest in the growing Christian consciousness of Jews and Judaism, a developing defense of the State of Israel, and maturing commitment to end all forms of prejudice and discrimination (social and emotional) implies a Jewish obligation to be involved in discussions with Christians. We post-Holocaust Jews are asked by a maturing Christianity to participate in the tremendous discoveries that dialogue brings about. Our previous participation, on both the local and national levels, makes it obvious that, as far as dialogue is concerned, *there are not enough Jews to go around*.

The ultimate aim of dialogue is to create and expand the operative notion of dignity in diversity. It is in the best interest of Jews and

Christians, and ultimately every citizen, to practice an informed pluralism, not merely to tacitly profess pluralism. Given these three facts -- the necessity of Jews, the commitment of Jews to education, and the ways and means of pluralism -- our most important task would seem to be to more gingerly define and walk the line between recognizing evil and recognizing friends.

Emil Fackenheim has said that the Nazis "murdered Jews if they had one Jewish grandparent, Christians only if they choose to be saints" (Fackenheim, 1978, 57). We ought to read this statement in terms of how Christianity originally understood the term saint: The Nazis chose to exterminate Christians only when they choose to be *Christians*! If so, what we Jews have to fear is not Christianity, nor discussions with Christians concerning our common (even if not agreed upon) interests. What we have to fear are self-professing Christians who are not in fact Christians. Although this enters the terrain of defining what Christianity is, a task which a contemporary Jewish author has not yet attempted, it does seem cogent that we Jews may engage in discussions which serve to point out our similarities as well as our differences. We Jews have never had anything to fear from the saints of the nations. It seems reasonable, in these terms, that we have an obligation to discuss what "saintliness" means. Jews do not claim to have saints. We do, however, claim to know *mensches*.

NOTES

1. The name means nothing. I randomly hit several keys at once on the keyboard of the word processor.

2. This statement is a quote of Fackenheim agreeing with Roy Eckardt's assessment, op. cit. p. 280.

3. Fackenheim speaks in another paper, "Was Hitler's War Just Another German War? A Post-Mortem on Bitburg," op. cit., p. 365, of a German friend's young adulthood, "a sincere democrat and anti-Nazi," who "was killed on the Russian front, fighting Hitler's war."

4. An extended commentary on this statement appears in "Holocaust Education" (The Social Justice Review, Sept./Oct., 1989, vol. 80, no. 9-10, pp. 156-160).

Chapter 12

Scratch a Goy

"If you live in New York City or any other big city, you are Jewish! It doesn't matter even if you're a Catholic. If you live in Butte, Montana, you're going to be Goyish even if you are Jewish.

Kool-aid is Goyish... Chocolate is Jewish...

-Lenny Bruce

The Jewish Liturgy

During a discussion of Christian liturgical teachings against Jews and Judaism, a participant showed anger at the one-sidedness of the discussion. The participant wanted to know why we were not also talking about Jewish liturgical teachings against Christians and Christianity. The simple answer, of course, is that there are no Jewish teachings in our liturgy against other religions. Jewish worship does not include, nor in any way necessitate, defamation of others. The rabbis, to be sure, had some uncomplimentary statements to make against pagan idolaters, but we may assume that these pagans are not currently present to complain. Nor were such statements ever popularized in the synagogue service. Again, the Talmud is replete with uncomplimentary discussions, albeit hidden references, to the developing Christian community; but the Talmud is not a formalized aspect of Jewish worship and is, in fact, a largely unknown work. Further, the statements in question did not find their way into Jewish liturgy. It is as if the Jew, standing before God, has no concern to define Judaism against any other way of life. In our contemporary

121

world, however, we continually face those who are different than ourselves.

What was particularly distressing about the participant's question was the fact that the person making the query was a Lutheran minister. Here we have a trained seminarian who wanted to know if it was not also true that Jewish sermons or preaching and worship contained anti-Christian materials. One wondered if the simple explanation would have been enough to satisfy his complaint.

Indeed, attempting to answer the question would undoubtedly have led to a situation where we would have been compelled to suggest his question was not legitimate. One cannot argue on absence, as it were, unless the minister were invited to attend not one but several Jewish services. A single service would not be statistically significant to show that Jews do not preach an anti-Christian message. Nevertheless, in place of attending a great number of Jewish services, might we not expect that the seminary would have taught certain preparatory lessons to the minister? Can we not have expected a comparative religion course, for example, to have pointed out that Judaism pre-dates Christianity and that we Jews did not build in statements which would serve to boast our own (developing) theology as against that of the other? Again, can we not have expected a course of theology to have taught that theological statements are positive whereas derogatory statements are negative and, therefore, not theology?

On the other hand, the question was legitimate. The question was legitimate if only because it was a statement of bewilderment in search of a response. The question was legitimate if only because, for the moment at least, the minister was expressing a fear which Christian peoples may have, even if they have neither the language required to express the fear nor the opportunity to wonder about Jewish worship. When we engage in dialogue with other faiths we obviously reveal only the best about ourselves, and only hear the best about the other (or so we hope). Though we may leave such educational sessions with a new respect for the other, a renewed understanding that they are somewhat like us in their address to God or their human requirements, there may be some of us who leave with a nagging suspicion that we are not given the whole story. Indeed, we will never have *all* of the story, but we may sometimes feel that the plot-outline is not enough to satisfy us concerning the gory details. This is not to suggest we spend a great amount of time rehearsing our mea culpas aloud or in public. But there may be times when we want to know not only that the other is satisfied in his or her religion, like us, or healthy in his or her religion, as we are, but is also struggling to make sense of the world, the traditions and the literature which has been preserved since early days. We want to know they are similar to us even when they are different.

In contemporary society, Jews to not preach against Christians or Christianity. The statement may be made unequivalently and without hesitation. Should the minister walk into a synagogue, he would not hear anti-Christian statements. He would, of course, hear Rabbis sermonize against erroneous behavior in general, but these sins of commission and omission are rarely if ever related to identifiable Christian behavior. Again, a Rabbi may go so far as to speak against a particular individual, Jewish or Christian, but the remarks would not be made *because* the individual were a Jew or Christian. Indeed, the individual may seldom be named, may only be assumed, or perhaps "understood" to be a certain person and, in all likelihood, a public person, a newsworthy person. Also, a Rabbi may be quite outspoken about political issues, including separation of Church and State, but these are issues which although sometimes identified as "Jewish" or "Christian" are in fact social issues which either attract or repel a broad spectrum of people.

There may be a discussion of how the nations have treated the Jews historically, but these discussions do not necessarily denote Christian treatment of Jews. Ill-treatment also came from Muslims, Romans, Assyrians, ancient Egyptians, and so on. There is discussion of the Holocaust, but rather than blame Christians per se, or even Germans per se, there is a marked tendency to personalize the horror to "what Hitler did." Similarly, there is a tendency to personalize to "what Stalin did," or "what Titus, Balak, Haman, or Pharaoh did." In such discussions it may be generally be deduced that each of these instances of terrible treatment distinctly do not represent "Christian," nor even "human," behavior.

Further, there may be direct comparison of Jewish and Christian ideology. For example, general statements such as "Jews do not practice asceticism" may be uttered. These statements may imply, or may be understood to imply, that Christians do practice asceticism. An honest commentator, however, would go on to point out that not all, nor even a majority, of Christians engage in such practice. Also some Jews, some Hasidic sects, for example, do practice forms of asceticism.   Our rabbis are rather given to avoiding mention of particular, and what may be termed "obvious," Christian doctrines (such as the Trinity or the resurrection of Jesus himself; although resurrection in general may be a topic of the sermon).   Again, a rabbi may choose to say something about the difference between literal acceptance of a text and "midrashic" acceptance of a text, and it may be   understood that Christians are implied (but surely not all Christians), and therefore the rabbis need not specifically state (the erroneous remark) that this is "a Christian trait."   Nor, because most behavior is a common human trait of our society, or a generally known trait of our society, need it be specifically stated that the rabbi is not referring to Christians.   In other words, direct comparisons of ideology, whether in a complete manner or a brief form, serves only for the rabbi to tell his or her congregants what he, she, or Judaism believes, and how he or she thinks his/her congregants should act.

Comparisons, finally, need not be derogatory. Whether one person or group believes Isaiah was a real person who had a real inspiration as opposed to the collective writings of two, three or four editorial voices does not effect our concern to live according to the principles espoused in the book which exists in his name.   Not all issues, however, are as neutral as this one may be. In fact, this may be the exception rather than the rule. It *does* seem to make a difference, for example, whether one believes the Bible is the literal word of God or the interpretative word atop a human intuition, insight, or impression. In itself the issue may not mean much but, insofar as religion is concerned with the ultimate interrelation of all phenomenon, the discussion of this issue cannot be allowed to be merely abstract. The issue of revelation *or* insight would seem to effect, for example, our manageability of the documents. If we cannot change, interpret or reapply any particular statement, then we do seem limited to comparisons between "what is true, because it says so" and what is creatively decided by "the community."

Nevertheless, it is a generally acceptable statement that Rabbis do not speak about Christianity in a negative manner.   This is an extremely commendable situation inasmuch as Rabbis by and large speak as individuals, and do not follow a pre-programmed lectionary of messages to be delivered or platforms to be espoused. There are, of course, the stable urgings for contributions to Jewish Federations (and philanthropy in general), support for the State of Israel (and democracy in general), and so on. Absence of anti-Christian messages from individual sermons is all the more surprising when you consider that anti-Christian broadcasts are not built into the structure of Jewish worship. Where is our hedge against assimilation? Or is it the case that precisely *because* the worship structure does not call for anti-Christian announcements that our Rabbis are compelled neither to revise them nor ignore them (which was the issue facing the group which met to discuss the structured "anti-Judaism" in the Christian liturgy)? If the latter is the case, and I think it is, our hedge against assimilation occurs by utterance of the positive, nurturing virtues of Judaism and a Jewish way of life. This stands in direct contrast to the intuitively dysfunctional comparisons which occur in a negative manner among some people. These negative comparisons seem to rely on the existence of a wrong in order to espouse the "right," a false in order to know "the true." Such negative comparisons seems self-defeating and contradictory. They are self-defeating because they require the other as a stooge against which to define the self. Hence, as much time and energy is expended upon the wrong as upon the right, with the possible result that the wrong will be advertised. Negative comparisons seem contradictory if only because when exacerbated they require the elimination of "the wrong" upon which their own "right" has been established and supported. In any event, there is neither a formal nor an informal need for Jews to disparage Christians or Christianity in the liturgy and therefore neither a formal nor informal need for Jews to be concerned to excise anti-Christian passages, messages or notations. You cannot excise what does not exist in print. Jews do not liturgically engage in anti-Christian diatribe. Case closed!

The Jewish Kopf

We Jews do, however, have a much more malicious method of engaging in anti-Christian rhetoric. While not structured in our liturgical worship, and very nearly strictly forbidden on the pulpits, our anti-Christian announcements are clear enough in our street-talk. While we note, even brag, that our worship does not rest on defamation of others, we do not hesitate to assert our superiority in terms of intelligence (both practical and abstract) and moral steadfastness. While we daven, "The evil eye, the evil inclination, and hatred of his fellow-creature drive a man out of the world" (Aboth II:16), we are concerned that our eye and inclination preserve our superiority at the expense of some fellow human beings. We boost ourselves higher by identifying those who are lower than us. Yet if the people above whom we propel ourselves are as lowly and depraved as we allow in our street-talk, they deserve our sympathy and support as an act of charity. There can be no doubt that the people in question are Christians, the dominant members of society (although a case can be made that not all those who profess to be Christians are so, that there are instances where baptism "did not take").

I do not need to investigate the historical background to the particular practices of asserting intellectual and moral superiority which I intend to discuss. No doubt we Jews have always felt ourselves better than the people who surrounded us: better than the Pharaohs, better than the Hamans, the Titus', the Stalins and Hitlers. Naturally superior. But this understates the case. We have seen that it may be thought necessary for a people to design themselves as superior to those who are not like them. In the case of minorities, designations of superiority will be more overt. Majorities, too, however, have the tools with which to tell themselves that they are doing something correct. There is an abject case where members of the dominant society will overtly claim superiority in a malicious manner. I am thinking, for example, of Skinheads and other white supremacists. You may argue that these types are not a majority, that they detract from the majority when they engage in openly prejudicial or violent behavior. Indeed, we assume the majority is silent, is blandly willing to live out the conviction that it is "doing something right." We only become outraged when the silence becomes filled with assertions of their "right doing." Thus, Skinheads assert themselves as "right," and this offends in part because their right conflicts with our own "right."

In the same manner, we are by and large willing to allow Christian peoples their own worship, and become upset at their worship if and when it impinges upon our assertions of right. Thus we find Christian liturgy problematic when in its structure it asserts a superiority over Jews and Judaism. The textual assertions and implications that "Jews killed Christ," for example, are repulsive. The commentary of Christian fathers and theologians that the Jews are despised and rejected by God is appalling. The inherent suggestion that Jews are damned and bound for everlasting torment in hell is obnoxious. If the truth be known, we are perfectly willing to let Christians worship in any manner they please as long as their worship does not infringe upon our own notion of ourselves, and does not have an adverse public effect, that is, does not spill over into social relations. The problem, of course, is that Christian behavior does fall into the public realm. The reason is that Christians, like Jews, by and large claim that religion is not a Sunday-only event, not something you can put on and take off at will, but a "way of life." What we object to is the quotation of biblical proof-texts which, taken out of context, intend to show that Jews are foul, inhuman creatures. We object to the antisemitic nuance of news reports, and the most "insignificant" disfiguring remarks on sitcoms. And we cannot be said to be wrong to be dissatisfied at these events.

What is interesting about our reactions in general is that we do not consider Christianity unless and until it impinges negatively upon us. The result is that we have a general perspective of Christianity as a negative impingement. We do not consider that the Christian religion may be -- indeed, certainly is -- a positive force for millions of people. While I have suggested that every people has a natural inclination to assert that what they are "doing right," this does not automatically exclude recognition of what other people are doing which, while it is not what we do, is right for them. This formulation does not necessarily require a cultural relativistic understanding. People simply do different things: like sleep on their back, or their side, or their stomach. We only become upset when the different things people do or say is suggested as the appropriate manner for every person to act. Relativism is an issue when either or both ways are perceived to be essential to intellectual or moral absolutes. If sleeping on one's side is absolutely the correct way to sleep, then the assertion that sleeping on one's back is proper spins us into a relativistic world. In a fair comparison of Judaism and Christianity, however, while we do things differently, the "goal" is similar. It may be the case that the "goal" is variously stated -- to serve and worship God, to live the best life possible, or to preserve the integrity of the human race. Yet each of these designations ultimately mean: to be the best I/we, can be as I/we perceive the needs of the moment. Tradition is important as a way of monitoring and modifying the moment (and religions become stagnant and die when the monitoring function severely overrides the *modifying* function).

As a subsidiary of the above, we become angry when we perceive that Christians boast Christianity as if over the bones of Judaism. This is known to have occurred, for example, when prophetic assertions of a self-recriminating nature for a specific time and place were taken as universal truths of a ubiquitous nature, that is, when in-house self-criticisms are taken out of context and applied to all the Jewish people of all times.   We object to universal assertions in such a manner precisely *because* they are not universally true.   We also object to relativistic assertions; as we should.   However, our own participation in such relativistic behavior parading in the form of universal assertions is much more malicious.   The reason is precisely because our form of denigration is not structured in the liturgy, is *not* a formalized process which, as a formal process, could be investigated, excised and corrected.   Our more malicious method of anti-Christian rhetoric, however, ought to be pointed out as an equally invalid way of making universal assertions in an identical manner as we object to in Christian liturgy spilling over into the public realm.   Indeed, our own form of this behavior originated in the public realm, in street-talk.

Because we do not consider Christianity as a religious or even a social phenomenon unless and until it impinges negatively on our own self-conceptualization, we make two atrocious statements of attitude, one intellectual and one involving moral consistency.   Ironically, as will be seen, our boast of intellectual superiority in the form in which it is tendered in the public realm shows the speakers not quite intellectually sound.   Likewise, our boast of moral consistency indicates that, at least in this one instance, we are neither moral nor consistent.   Intellectually, we boast that we do not have, that others *do* have, "a goyishe kopf" ("kopf" is Yiddish for "head").   Morally, we boast our consistent social behavior, in this case our pride of Jewishness, by saying that if you scratch a goy, you find an antisemite.

The notion of a "goyishe kopf" may mean anything from an unspecified way of non-Yiddishkeit muddled thinking to a specific Christian mind-set.   To have a goyishe manner of thinking has, of course, its antimony: a Jewish manner of thinking.   But a goyish or Jewish manner of thinking is not all which is enveloped in the notion of a goyishe kopf.   The phrase also assumes Jewish values.   So, for example, to save money for the college education of one's children indicates the presence of a Jewish kopf, whereas not to plan ahead for this eventuality indicates a goyishe kopf.   As this single example may indicate it is quite possible for a Christian to have a Jewish kopf (i.e., a Jewish head on his or her shoulders, Jewish values) and just as likely that a Jewish individual may have a goyishe kopf.   Perhaps the statement that certain non-Jewish people, known to the speaker, have a Jewish kopf (i.e., spend money on books rather than gadgets, show more concern for nutritious food than fancy cars, buy educational toys) is our version of saying "some of my best friends are..." However, when someone with a goyishe kopf says "Some of my best friends are Jewish," he or she at least recognizes the Jew as a separate entity. When we say a non-Jew has a Jewish kopf, we assimilate them into Judaism. The issue is, or should be, whether individuals and groups have cogent and efficacious human values or not. The values in question need not necessarily be my own. Different people may do something different and, as a consequence, do it better. We Jews recognize our tradition as the source for human values. When we recognize non-Jews as possessing a similar value-system, we assume they have a Jewish head on their shoulders.

Certainly to say of a fellow Jew that he or she has a goyishe kopf is the ultimate put-down. The phrase in this context is a disclaimer that one's fellow Jew is indeed one's fellow. As such, it is a denial of *avodah Yisroel*, the unqualified love of one Jew for another simply for the fact that the other is a Jew. *Avodah Yisroel* is a major premise of a Jewish kopf. However, if a term is useful for designating a certain type of behavior, it ought to be the case that the same term not deny the very same behavior while it is in use. Yet if "Jewish kopf" is applicable to both Jews and non-Jews -- thereby suggesting the term is not useful for designating a specific type of behavior -- then the antinomous phrase "goyishe kopf," which is also applicable to both Jews and non-Jews, ought not deny the major premise of *avodah Yisroel*. But it does! Hence, we may conclude that the phrase "goyishe kopf" is not only not explanatory, but is contradictory. The phrase is not only not descriptive, it cannot be made to be descriptive. Anyone who uses such a term cannot be very practical.

When we say someone has a "goyishe kopf," we ought to recognize we are engaging in offensive behavior. It does not matter that we do not make the accusations *to* someone we *believe* has a "goyishe kopf." Like everything else which occurs on the street, eventually everyone knows about it. More importantly, in making the accusation, we substantiate *our* attitude that the world is composed of types. We assume that one type, for example, enjoys working as a mechanic while another, superior type, enjoys working for the future of their children. Placing the distinction in this manner, I hope, indicates the foolishness of the accusation that another has a "goyishe kopf." We cannot be certain the mechanic does not labor with his or her children in mind. We cannot even be certain he or she wants to be a mechanic. All we are doing is making illicit value judgements. We assume a person *is* his or her job. We further assume that the job defines the person, and that the person has no valuable existence beyond the workplace. Perhaps this is why we think we are making ontological assessments when, in fact, we are not even making valid (well reasoned, verifiable) statements of fact.

Not only are we not making cogent statements of fact, but focus on whatever truth content there is to our statement inclines to ignore the truth that facts change. The mechanic may be working his or her way through medical school The mechanic may be writing treatises in philosophy during his or her spare time. The mechanic, finally, may be happy and satisfied at their occupation. The mechanic may feel he or she is performing a valuable service when our automobile is repaired. Certainly *we* are thankful when someone we may identify as possessing a "goyishe kopf" (which has come to mean someone who is skilled with his or her hands) performs a service for us. The truth of the matter comes out when we say, "I wish I could have fixed this vehicle," or "I wish I could have built that book shelf."

The above discussion should at least indicate that one could both mend a hole in a fence at one point during the day and understand a text on child care at some other point, or assemble a basketball pole now and be philanthropic later. The fact that some people do not wish to do both or cannot do both may be a matter of personal inclination, a self-imposed limitation, or a genuine lack of skill. It would seem that a person who could both work with his or her hands and work with his or her mind, family, society would be more effective and, eventually, more helpful to others.

I am not arguing that there are not people with more or less common sense. Surely some people make better decisions than others. Perhaps those who do not make sensible life decisions -- but we have to distinguish between those who really cannot make coherent life decisions and those who simply do not make the decision we would have made if we were in their circumstance -- perhaps these people need instruction, or would benefit from developing foresight, or could learn from a good example. Perhaps they will require our assistance with food, clothing, or shelter. Indeed, the very best of Judaism,

Christianity, and Islam seem to agree that we ought to help one another, even our enemies. It does not matter whether the person we help is a fellow Jew, a Christian neighbor, or a heathen stranger. We delay the helping process, we impede recognition of those who require help, when we waste time making un-valuable distinctions of the world as we know it into an "us" and a "them." We ought to engage in creating the world as we envision it. If these people in question are so depraved, they deserve less our private ridicule than our public support. Again, substantiating a worldview that there are us and there are them will effect us in an "un-Jewish," non-beneficial manner.

To be told this discussion is "not that big a deal," or that it is a straw-man argument, seems simply to show how insidious the problem is.

Scratch a Goy

The notion that you may "scratch a goy," whatever its historical genesis, is a derivative of the Yiddish saying "*A goy blaybt a goy*" or, very loosely translated, "So what did you expect; this is the behavior you get from non-Jewish people." I call it a derivative because "scratch a goy" intimates an atmosphere of sophistication or development with which non-Jews are at least paying tribute to the idea of being tolerant, or considerate of difference. The implication is that the contemporary non-Jew is a veneer we see in the public realm and which, when scratched, reveals a hidden creature.

When we say "scratch a goy" in contemporary society, when the great majority of people we know besides fellow Jews are Christian -- none of them Palmyrenian pagans or Eleusinian cultists -- there is no doubt that we mean "scratch a Christian." Such an attitude invites the recrimination, "scratch a Jew and get an anti-Christian." Certainly such an attitude does not inspire the non-Jew to reassess his or her anti-Jewish feelings, does not show we *are* better because we do not engage in such merely attitudinal practices. Indeed, all we do is indicate that we are engaging in precisely the behavior we are decrying.

"Scratch a goy" is offensive not only because of what it implies as universal depravity, but of what it says about the Jewish perspective of our non-Jewish neighbors. The statement not only projects a depraved world-view but allows us to participate in the corrupt world while implying our superiority to it. Surely if you scratch a Jew you will not come up with anything so deranged and horrendous as an antisemite. Yet our boast of superiority at the same time substantiates the world of antisemitism. If there were no goyim to scratch, how would we know our superiority? It would be better if we could base our natural inclination to tell what we *are* "doing right" on what we are doing right, and not on what other people are doing wrong.

If we were really to believe that if you "scratch a goy" you will reveal an antisemite, I would have to believe that my clerical acquaintance was antisemitic. Given my knowledge of his concern for revising both Christian liturgy and the popular perspective of Jews and Judaism, his remorse over Christian treatment of Jews in the past, and his generally philanthropic disposition, this claim cannot be made. If we were really to believe the "scratch a goy" legend, I would have to believe that seething below the surface of every non-Jew was a flame of molten hatred ready to erupt with the least provocation. If we were really to believe "scratch a goy," I would have to believe that anyone with squinted eyes was a murderer of Jews. I would, that is, have to be paranoid and prejudiced to the extreme. But are not paranoia and extreme prejudice the calling cards of antisemitism?

Scratch a goy and get an antisemite (but what if the person in question has a depth of Jewish kopf)? The issues become unclear. But again, scratch anyone deep enough and you will find revolt against irritation, belligerency, a will not to be scratched, and a scratching in return. What are we Jews doing scratching anyone anyway? Is not one of our boasts, as a most democratic and tolerant people, that we have so few prejudices? Of course, sometimes the boast that we have no prejudices means that we regard such thoughts as truths.

I have never perceived anti-Christian sentiments in the Jewish liturgy, nor heard them from sermons in any synagogue I have ever attended. I have, in fact, heard several rabbis say many significant things about Christian individuals, Christians in general, and even Christianity. Christianity is a moral force in the world, and this is how the Church is treated in our contemporary literature and in our heuristic remarks. Anti-Christian sentiments are found in our street-talk, that talk wherein we are not seriously concerned about what we are "doing right" but about how we seem to be doing right only in comparison with another's seeming wrong-headedness.

I suggest we talk in a negative manner about Christianity because we do not have a positive handle with which to approach the issue of the dominant majority. I repeat the following remark in the spirit of dialogical clarity, that is, the lucidity which comes from knowing that both Jews and Christians in contemporary society are trying to find their separate renewal in the togetherness of conversation. In this post-Holocaust era, we live in a unique situation. We have survived a pagan effort to thoroughly *rid* the world of Jews. Although there are yet pockets of Hitlerism which assume, and act, as if one living Jew is far too many, we are fortified by the efforts of the Catholics who work through the offices of ecumenical affairs, and the Protestants who work through their various offices of interfaith relations. With the growing Christian consciousness of the worth and dignity of Jews, the increasing appreciation of the educational benefits of diversity, we have come upon a time where there is a Christian commitment to the idea that there are *not enough* Jews to go around. There are not enough Jews, that is, who are willing to respond in similarly tolerant, critically studied, and openly faithful ways to the Christian phenomenon. There are, if I may venture one more in-house assessment, not enough Jews committed to the practical and beneficial engagement of the Jewish kopf.

Appendices

Passages alluded to in the body of the paper entitled "Jews and Catholics Discussing Bible and Jesus" are reprinted from The New English Bible with the Apocrypha: Study Edition.

A. Luke 2:21:

"Eight days later the time came to circumcise him, and he was given the name Jesus, the name given by the angel before he was conceived."

B. Luke 2:41-47:

"Now it was the practice of his parents to go to Jerusalem every year for the Passover festival; and when he was twelve, they made the pilgrimage as usual. When the festive season was over and they started for home, the boy Jesus stayed behind in Jerusalem. His parents did not know of this; but thinking that he was with the party they journeyed on for a whole day, and only then did they begin looking among their friends and relations. As they could not find him they returned to Jerusalem to look for him; and after three days they found him sitting in the temple surrounded by the teachers, listening to them and putting questions; and all who heard him were amazed at his intelligence and the answers he gave."

C. Matthew 6:9-13:

"Our Father in heaven,
thy name be hallowed;
thy kingdom come,
thy will be done,
on earth as it is in heaven.
Give us today our daily bread.
Forgive us the wrong we have done,
as we forgive those who have wronged us.

And do not bring us to the test,
but save us from the evil one."

D. John 2:13-17:

"As it was near the time of the Jewish Passover, Jesus went up to
Jerusalem. There he found in the temple the dealers in cattle, sheep
and pigeons, and the money-changers seated at their tables. Jesus
made a whip of cords and drove them out of the temple, sheep,
cattle, and all. He upset the tables of the money-changers,
scattering their coins. Then he turned on the dealers in pigeons:
'Take them out,' he said; 'you must not turn my Father's house into
a market.'"

E. Acts 4:11-12:

"This Jesus is the stone rejected by the builders which has become
the keystone - and you [the Jewish rulers, elders and doctors of the
law] are the builders. There is no salvation in anyone else at all,
for there is no name under heaven granted to men, by which we
may achieve salvation."

F. The following passage is included as a suggestion for an example of
a more severe anti-Jewish statement. Although not handed out for
discussion, I believe an exchange of ideas on this passage would
have been more beneficial than Acts 4:11-12. In the above passage,
the anti-Jewish elements are camouflaged behind a theologically
abstract statement. Although I can appreciate why the leaders of the
dialogue may not have wanted to distribute persuasive anti-Jewish
statements, I cannot understand why a discussion of antisemitism
would have to be constructed on the passage from Acts which is
theologically internal to the Christian community. If the goal of
discussing antisemitism or suggestions of anti-Judaism in order to
recognize and rout the disease, the goal would have been more
cogently accomplished by a passage where the disease is clearly
evidenced, as in John 8:44-47 where Jesus claims the Jewish people
are of the devil. Whereas the previous passage merely implied that
the Jews (temporarily) rejected 'the stone,' and placed emphasis on
the uniqueness of Jesus, the following passage clearly, redundantly,
places the emphasis on the supposed evil nature of the Jews
themselves: "Your father is the devil and you choose to carry out
your father's desires. He was a murderer from the beginning, and
is not rooted in the truth; there is no truth in him. When he tells a
lie he is speaking his own language, for he is a liar and the father
of lies ... You are not God's children...."

Bibliography

Arendt, Hannah. The Jew as Pariah: Jewish Identity and Politics in the Modern Age. New York: Grove Press, 1978.

Augustine. On Christian Doctrine. Translated by D.W. Robertson, Jr. New York: Library of Liberal Arts [Macmillan Publishing Co.], 1987.

Baeck, Leo. The Essence of Judaism. New York: Schocken Books, 1970.

-----. Judaism and Christianity. New York: Atheneum, 1970.

Bateson, Greegory. Mind and Nature. New York: Bantam, 1980.

Barnstone, Willis, ed. The Other Bible. San Francisco: Harper and Row, 1984.

Batstone, David B. "The Transformation of the Messianic Idea in Judaism and Christianity in Light of the Holocaust: Reflections on the Writing of Elie Wiesel" in Journal of Ecumenical Studies 23:4 (pp.587-600), Fall 1986.

Bauer, Walter, Orthodoxy and Heresy in Earliest Christianity. Philadelphia: Fortress Press, 1971.

Bauer, Yehuda. They Chose Life. New York: The American Jewish Committee, 1973.

Baum, Gregory. Is the New Testament Anti-Semitic? New York: Paulist Press, 1965.

Bergman, Samuel H. Faith and Reason: Modern Jewish Thought. New York: Schocken Books, 1968.

Bokser, Ben Zion. Pharisaism in Transition. New York: Bloch Publishing Company, 1935.

Bonhoeffer, Dietrich. Letter and Papers from Prison, edited by Ebergard Bethge. New York: Macmillan Publishing Co., 1971.

Bruman, Ursula. American Thought and Religious Typology. Rutgers: Rutgers University Press, 1970.

Buber, Martin. Two Types of Faith. New York: Harper and Row, 1961.

-----. Between Man and Man. New York: Macmillan Publishing Co., 1972.

Bultmann, Rudolf. Jesus and the Word. New York: Charles Scribner's Sons, 1958.

Craveri, Marcello. The Life of Jesus. New York: Grove Press, Inc., 1967.

Crossan, John Dominic. "Divine Immediacy and Human Immediacy: Towards a New First Principle in Historical Jesus Research" in Semeia 44, 1988, pp.121-140.

Engel, Mary Potter and Walter E. Wyman, editors. Revisioning the Past: Prospects in Historical Theology. Minneapolis: Fortress Press, 1983.

Fackenheim, Emil L. Quest for Past and Future: Essays in Jewish Theology. Boston: Beacon Press, 1968.

-----. God's Presence in History. New York: Harper and Row, 1972.

-----. The Jewish Return Into History: Reflections in the Age of Auschwitz and a New Jerusalem. New York: Schocken Books, 1978.

-----. To Mend the World. New York: Schocken Books, 1982.

-----. The Jewish Thought of Emil Fackenheim, edited by Michael L. Morgan. Detroit: Wayne State University Press, 1987.

Falk, Harvey. Jesus and the Pharisees: A New Look at the Jewishness of Jesus. New York: The Paulist Press, 1985.

Feeley-Harnik, Gillian. The Lord's Table. Philadelphia: University of Pennsylvania press, 1981.

Flannery, Edward H. The Anguish of the Jews. New York: Macmillan Publishing Co., 1979.

Fox, G. George. The Jews, Jesus, and the Christ. New York: Augus Books, 1953.

Franck, Frederick. "The Cosmic Fish," in Cross Currents, Fall 1986, Vol. XXXVI, no.3, pp.285-293.

Gibbs, Robert. Correlations in Rosenzweig and Levinas. Princeton: Princeton University Press, 1992.

Glatzer, Nahum. Franz Rosenzweig: His Life and Thought. New York: Schocken Books, 1953.

Glueck, Nelson. Hesed in the Bible. Cincinnati: Hebrew Union College Press, 1967.

Goldberg, Michael. Jews and Christians: Getting Our Stories Straight. Nashville: Abingdon, 1965.

-----. Theology and Narrative. Nashville: Abingdon, 1982.

Goldstein, Morris. Jesus in the Jewish Tradition. New York: KTAV Publishing House, Inc., 1950.

Hagner, Donald. The Jewish Reclamation of Jesus. Grand Rapids, Academie Books, 1984.

Halevi, Judah. The Kuzari: An Argument for the Faith of Israel. New York: Schocken Books, 1974.

Hall, Stuart George. Melito of Sardis on Pascha. Cambridge: Oxford University Press, 1975.

Hartman, Geoffrey and Sanford Budick. Midrash and Literature. New Haven: Yale University Press, 1986.

Hengel, Martin. The Charismatic Leader and His Followers. New York: Crossroad Publications Company, 1981.

Herberg, Will. Judaism and Modern Man. New York: Atheneum, 1951.

Herford, R. Travers. Christianity in Talmud and Midrash. London: Williams and Norgate, 1903.

-----. "The Influence of Judaism on Jews" in The Legacy of Israel. Oxford: Clarendon Press, 1927.

-----. Judaism in the New Testament Period. London: Lindsey, 1928.

-----, ed. Pirke Aboth: The Ethics of the Talmud: The Sayings of the Fathers. New York: Schocken Books, 1974.

Hopko, Thomas. "A Response to John Pawlikowski" in Auschwitz: Beginning of a New Era?, edited by Eva Fleischner. New York: KTAV Publishing House, Inc., 1977.

Imboden, Roberta. From the Cross to the Kingdom: Sartrean Dialectics and Liberation Theology. San Francisco: Harper and Row, 1987.

Jacob, Walter. Christianity Through Jewish Eyes: The Quest for Common Ground. Cincinnati: Hebrew Union College Press, 1974.

Kelly, Dean M. and Berhard E. Olsen. The Meaning and Conduct of Dialogue. New York: The National Conference of Christians and Jews, [n.d.].

Klausner, Joseph. Jesus of Nazareth. New York: Menorah Publications, 1979.

Koester, Helmut and James W. Robinson. Trajectories Through Early Christianity. Philadelphia: Fortress Press, 1971.

Kung, Hans. Theology for the Third Millennium: An Ecumenical View. Translated by Peter Heinegg. New York: Anchor Books, 1988.

Lapide, Pinchas. Israelis, Jews and Jesus. New York: Doubleday, 1979.

-----. The Resurrection of Jesus. Minneapolis: Augsburg Publishing House, 1983.

Lauterback, Jacob Z. Rabbinical Essays. Cincinnati: Hebrew Union College Press, 1951.

Lowry, Charles W. The First Theologians. Chicago: Gateway Editions, 1986.

Luther, Martin. Luther and the Jews. New York: Lutheran Council in the USA, 1983.

Maddox, Randy L. Toward an Ecumenical Fundamental Theology. Chico, Calif.: Scholars Press, 1984.

Moehlman, Conrad. The Christian-Jewish Tragedy. New York: Leo Hart, 1933.

Moore, George Foote. Judaism, 3 volumes. Cambridge: Harvard University Press, 1927.

Montifiore, Claude. Judaism and St. Paul. New York: E.P. Dutten and Company, 1915.

Neusner, Jacob. History and Torah. New York: Schocken Books, 1965.

-----. Telling Tales: Making Sense of Christian and Judaic Nonsense. The Urgency and Basis for Judeo-Christian Dialogue. Louisville: Westminster/John Knox Press, 1993.

Novak, David. Jewish-Christian Dialogue: A Jewish Justificiation. New York: Oxford University Press, 1989.

Orwell, George. A Collection of Essays. New York: Harcourt Brace Jovanovich, 1957.

Parkes, James. The Conflict of Church and Synagogue. New York: Harper and Row, 1053.

Pascal, Blasie. Pensees. Translated by A.J. Krailshermer. Middlesex: Penguin Books, 1975.

Patai, Raphael. The Jewish Mind. New York: Charles Scribner's Sons, 1977.

Pawlikowski, John T. "The Rejudaization of Christianity: Its Impact on the Church and Its Implications for the Jewish People," unpublished address to the Hebrew Union College in Jerusalem, February 1, 1988.

Rad, Gerhard von. Old Testament Theology, 2 volumes. New York: Harper and Row, 1965.

Rahner, Karl. Karl Rahner in Dialogue: Conversations and Interviews, 1965-1982. Edited by Paul Imhoff and Hubert Biallowans. New York: Crossroads Press, 1986.

-----. Karl Rahner: Theologian of the Graced Search for Meaning. Edited by Geffrey B. Kelly. Minneapolis: Fortress Press, 1993.

Richardson, Cyril C., editor. Early Christian Fathers. New York: Macmillan Publishing Co., 1970.

Rivkin, Ellis. The Shaping of Jewish History. New York: Charles Scribner's Sons, 1971.

-----. What Crucified Jesus. Nashville: Abingdon Press, 1974.

Rorty, Richard. Philosophy and the Mirror of Nature. Princeton: Princeton University Press, 1980.

Rosenzweig, Franz. Star of Redemption. Boston: Beacon Press, 1972.

Rosenzweig, Franz and Eugen Rosenstock-Huessy. Judaism Despite Christianity. New York: Schocken Books, 1971.

Rousseau, Richard W. Christianity and Judaism: The Deepening Dialogue. Montrose, Pa.: Ridge Row Press, 1983.

Rubenstein, Richard. After Auschwitz: Radical Theology and Contemporary Judaism. Indianapolis: Bobbs-Merrill, 1966.

-----. The Religious Imagination. Boston: Beacon Press, 1971.

-----. My Brother Paul. New York: Harper and Row, 1972.

Sandmel, Samuel. We Jews and Jesus. London: Oxford University Press, 1965.

-----. Two Living Traditions: Essays on Religion and the Bible. Detroit: Wayne State University Press, 1972.

-----, general editor of annotations and essays in: The New English Bible with the Apocrypha Study Edition. New York: Oxford University Press, 1975.

-----. Judaism and Christian Beginnings. London: Oxford University Press, 1978.

Schechter, Solomon. Aspects of Rabbinic Theology. New York: Schocken Books, 1972.

Schoenfield, Hugh J. According to the Hebrews. London: Duckworth, 1937.

-----. After the Cross. San Diego: A.S. Barnes, 1981.

-----. The Passover Plot. New York: Bantam Books, 1986.

Schurer, Emil. The Literature of the Jewish People in the Time of Jesus. New York: Schocken Books, 1972.

Schwartz, G. David. "Holocaust Education" in The Social Justice Review, September-October, 1989, vol. 80, no. 9-10, pp. 156-160.

-----. "As If Jesus and the Pharisees Were Developing Similarly and Simultaneously" in New Theology Review, Nov. 1991, vol. 4, no. 4, pp. 63-77.

Shermis, Michael and Arthur E. Zannoni, editors. Introduction to Jewish-Christian Relations. Mahwah, N.J.: Paulist Press, 1991.

Tillich, Paul. Dynamic of Faith. New York: Harper and Row, 1957.

-----. A History of Christian Thought. New York: Simon and Schuster, 1968.

-----. What Is Religion? New York: Harper and Row, 1973.

Tracy, David. The Analogical Imagination: Christian Theology and the Culture of Pluralism. New York: Crossroads, 1989.

Troki, Isaac. Faith Strengthened. Translated by Moses Mocatta. New York: KTAV Publishing House Inc., 1970.

Van Buren, Paul M. Discerning the Way. Philadelphia: Westminster Press, 1982.

-----. A Christian Theology of the People Israel. San Francisco: Harper and Row, 1987.

-----. Christ in Context. San Francisco: Harper and Row, 1988.

Vermes, Geza. Jesus the Jew. New York: Macmillan Publishing Co., 1974.

Weiss-Rosmarin, Trude. Judaism and Christianity: The Differences. New York: Jonathan David, 1972.

Wise, Isaac M. The Martyrdom of Jesus of Nazareth. New York: Bloch Publishing and Printing Company, 1888.

Wolfson, Harry Austryn. Religious Philosophy: A Group of Essays. New York: Atheneum, 1965.

Zeitlin, Solomon. Who Crucified Jesus? New York: Bloch Publishing Co., 1964.

Name Index

About the Author

G. David Schwartz lives in Cincinnati, Ohio with his wife, Gilda, and children: Sara, Michelle and Dan. A graduate of Miami University (of Ohio) with a degree in philosophy, Schwartz is a freelance author. His works have appeared in The Journal of Ecumenical Studies, The New Theology Review, The Social Justice Review, Encounter, and elsewhere. Schwartz is active in several Cincinnati area Jewish-Christian dialogue groups.